The Christian Challenge Series
Edited by ASHLEY SAMPSON

THE MASTERY OF EVIL

by
ROGER LLOYD
Canon of Winchester

THE CENTENARY PRESS
37 ESSEX STREET, STRAND, LONDON

First Published, February 1941
Reprinted, June 1942

PRINTED IN GREAT BRITAIN BY THE WHITEFRIARS PRESS LTD.
LONDON AND TONBRIDGE

AUTHOR'S NOTE

AN article which appeared first in the pages of the *Quarterly Review* is reprinted, almost in its entirety, in Chapter V; and I must acknowledge with gratitude the permission of the Editor. Embedded in Chapter VII are some paragraphs from a sermon preached before the University of Cambridge in April, 1939.

R. L.

CONTENTS

CHAPTER I

THE PRESSURE OF EVIL

WE are drawing close to the end of perhaps the most calamitous decade the world has ever seen. It begins with the bursting of the great economic blizzard upon the world, and it ends with the defeat of France and the threat of still more trials to come. Its middle years see the advent of Nazism to power in Germany, and during its course no less than eleven free nations have been reduced to total servitude. Nor is there much reason to doubt that these eleven will soon be followed by further victims. In all history it would be difficult to find a more uniformly disastrous span of ten years. Of what all this has entailed in terms of human misery, and chaos of every kind, it is useless to speak. As much of this story as the human consciousness is capable of taking in—and that no doubt is but a small fraction of the whole—is told every day for us by our newspapers. All these things press heavily on our spirits day by day, and for ten years we have endured them. But under and beneath this pressure there lies another still more heavy. It is the realisation of the overwhelming power and drive of evil. We feel that we are the first of many generations to understand what Jesus meant when he said, " This is your hour and the power of darkness." An earlier generation of biblical scholars may have been embarrassed by the Little Apocalypse in St. Mark's Gospel; today our embarrassment is of a different, sterner kind, for we have watched it happen :

When ye see the abomination of desolation, spoken of by Daniel the prophet, standing where it ought not, (let him that readeth understand,) then let them that be in Judæa flee to the mountains : and let him that is on the housetop not go down into the house, neither enter therein, to take anything out of his house : and let him that is in the field not turn back again for to take up his garment. But woe to them that are with child, and to them that give suck in those days. And pray ye that your flight be not in the winter. For in those days shall be affliction, such as was not from the beginning of the creation which God created unto this time, neither shall be. And except the Lord had shortened those days, no flesh should be saved.

(Mark xiii. 14–20)

We read the warning and feel as though Jesus was speaking across the centuries to His disciples of 1940.

The positive achievements of evil, even if we arbitrarily limit the term to the sweep of the totalitarian scourge, are frankly astonishing even to those who never entertained any optimistic theories about the waning powers of the devil and the inevitability of human progress. The optimists, of course, are simply dumbfounded. For of them evil has made a bitter sport. It has taken all the instruments of progress proclaimed as sufficient by Buckle and all his latter-day humanist followers, and made them one and all serve its own reactionary purpose. The growth of scientific knowledge operating upon technical inventions, the stimulated fertility of the soil, the increased availability of raw materials, and the swift spread of universal education were to produce an applied intelligence by which man was bound to save himself, and to build at last the social kingdom of his immemorial dreams. Instead, evil has taken one and all of these things and turned them into scourges. All were potentially the instruments of the good, and all have in actuality become the means of the good's destruction. Today there is hardly one of us who would not burn up every drop of oil in every well in the world if only he had the chance. Evil has taken multitudes of decent young men and turned them into devils, their sisters applauding the progress. It has largely corrupted the most elementary forms of expression of the human spirit, such as bravery, patriotism and love, and made of them instruments to procure the collapse of one stronghold after another where they were still allowed a normal scope. Fouling the well of truth, it has forced the statesmen of every nation where truth was still valued to play fast and loose with moral truth, as the lamentable diplomatic history of the Western Democracies during the last ten years shows plainly. It has been a bitter thing to watch our statesmen refraining their policies from righteousness, calling wickedness expedient and so conniving at its growth, and shaking hands with murder. The war, we had thought, would at least mean an end of humbug in high places, and to that extent we welcomed it. Yet even there we were mistaken, as the record of French politics since September, 1939, shows. There is as yet no release from evil.

It is in such circumstances that Christians today have to proclaim the Gospel—the Good News of man's release from sin through Jesus Christ. The very starkness of the situation, with all its complications reduced to the elements of their revolutionary simplicities, makes that task the easier. None can doubt the Gospel's relevance, even if many doubt its power. Yet even the grimmest and most realistic assessment of the facts of evil's power should not make us doubt the corresponding power of God through us to master evil and destroy it. That is a task for which the whole range of history is not finally sufficient, but it is also a process which this present generation has the chance to carry many stages further than come within the scope of most generations. To deny this is not only to show a poor trust in God. It is also to have made a faulty, incomplete analysis of the facts. As a nation in arms we do not doubt our power to defeat the enemy. A survey of our respective military strengths might reasonably make us quail, but it does not. We have even less reason to doubt that we have the power to gain the mastery over both public and private evil.

To do this we must not waste our time or our energy in railing against God for allowing evil to exist. The problem of why evil is continually allowed to spoil the world over which God reigns, and in which nothing happens as apart from His will, is the oldest problem of all and the least soluble. Many answers to the riddle have been suggested, but none is wholly satisfactory. The writers of the four Gospels made no attempt to answer it, though the problem was certainly pre-

sent to their minds as they wrote. In his pro-
logue, St. John deliberately raises it in its most
acute form. " All things were made by him ; and
without him was not anything made that was
made." But he does not stay to answer it, for
the whole story he is about to tell is the answer.
It is God's answer, and in His answer God wastes
no time in explaining what He is about, but
instead shows how evil may be overcome, and
that is the Good News.

Nor must the Christian allow himself to be
shocked by this present revelation of evil's power.
To a Christian nothing can ever be purely shock-
ing, because to be shocked is to be betrayed into a
waste of energy and to be stripped of the power
to help. A priest who hears confessions, or deals
in other ways with distressed human souls which
lay themselves bare for God's healing through
him, knows very well that he must never be
shocked, must never even show surprise, no
matter what he hears or from whom he hears it.
If he shows so much as a glimmer of either shock
or surprise he has already forfeited all his power
to help. So it is when we are thinking of evil on
the rather more impersonal scale of its attack on
humanity as a whole. There, too, the same conditions of effectiveness hold good. In any case,

Christians who have allowed themselves to be shocked into numbness by the events of the last ten years cannot have been reading their Bibles lately; or at least cannot have been regarding the principles laid down in the scriptures as always and everywhere binding and relevant. They cannot, that is to say, have been treating their bibles as Bibles. For the Bible is a book about evil no less than about good. It begins with the myth of the subtle and malevolent serpent. The Psalmist breaks his heart in a dozen places over the distressing nearness and power of evil, only a little less present to his consciousness than God Himself. In the Gospels Jesus accepts evil as a fact to be fought. He is never surprised by it : such surprise as He shows is only over men's lack of faith, which involves them in a fatalistic acquiescence in evil when they might be defeating it if only they had faith. The Bible ends with a riot of apocalyptic imagery when the Book of Life is opened by the Lamb, and out of it emerge the Four Horsemen of Conquest, Fratricidal Quarrel, Siege and Death. These things must come out of the Book of Life because they are there. Human history contains them, and in all periods which lie under the judgment of the Lamb, and in which that judgment is made apparent, out they must come into the open to ravage and destroy. To the Christian whose mind is steeped in the Bible the events of modern European history must be infinitely saddening, but not in the least surprising.

Nor, for him, should they be dismaying. We have gone through no worse road than the Jews in biblical days went through before us. We hardly could. They related their agonies to God, and therefore it was through them that the secret of the mastery over evil was given to the world. It is still there for us to use. Having put away horror, with its concomitant process of the numbed conscience, and surprise, the result of a faulty analysis of the facts, we must first learn to understand. How does evil work? Are there any laws which condition evil's growth and decline and by which the devil himself is bound? These are the kind of questions which need to be answered. Answering them, we can take the measure of the enemy. In a word, we must understand evil if we are to master it.

CHAPTER II

''OUT OF THE HEART''

THE test of any great moral teacher is the account that he gives of evil. If he deals with it only in its overt acts, murder, treachery, fraud, and war, his claims to greatness cannot stand much scrutiny. He must go far deeper than that, looking from the act to the motive, from the motive to the interior principle of corruption, and from this principle of corruption to the structure both of society and of life itself which contains and nourishes it. We naturally claim for our Lord that He is the greatest of all moral teachers, but we do so not, in the first instance, because we believe Him to be the incarnate Son of God, but because it is a matter of demonstrable fact that His view of evil penetrates more deeply into the heart of reality than the view of any other moral teacher who has ever lived.

"Out of the heart," He said, "proceed evil thoughts, murders, adulteries," and with them all other sins. They come out of the heart because they are there, and, being there, they are bound to come out in one form or another. Now a doctor may think of the heart as a physical engine for pumping blood round the human frame, and from this point of view it is neither more nor less important than the liver, the lungs, or certain glands. It is just one physical instrument among many others by the healthy co-operation of which the life of the body is maintained. The poet, the humanist and the theologian see the heart in an altogether different light. They think of it mystically as the source of an action and sacramentally as the root of perception. It is with our hearts that we like to think that we love and feel and move. The ancient prayer, " God be in my head and in my understanding," rises to a crescendo and ends in a climax, " God be in my heart and in my thinking." It occurs to very few to reflect that really the mind and not the heart is the instrument of understanding. Nor would any of us like the prayer to be re-written in the interests of physical correctitude. In common speech, in fact, the heart is a sacramental symbol. It is the outward and visible sign of the inward and spiritual force of life, and it stands for that spiritual focus of energy by which our conduct is directed.

Jesus, then, said of evil that it was a spiritual

phenomenon; and this, His understanding of evil, was a thing so fresh and it cut so deep that the publicans and sinners flocked to Him, because they felt that though they lived in a country abundantly supplied with moral teachers, only He really understood their trouble. He treated evil as a spiritual force, to be diagnosed by spiritual perception and treated by spiritual methods. This meant that He must imply two dangerous truths. (Everything He said was "dangerous," and that was not the least of the reasons for His crucifixion.) He was saying, in effect, that evil and good have a certain kinship, in that both are spiritual phenomena, and therefore both are subject to exactly the same laws of growth. This comes out in the Gospel, as also in the history of Christendom, in the way in which only the holy seemed really able to understand the mind of the chronic sinner, and those possessed by a devil were always the first to recognise Jesus for what He was. The danger of it is the heresy, which crops up again and again, of supposing that because good and evil are akin in their methods of conquest and the conditions of their growth, therefore they are two different aspects of the same reality, and so are all too easily taken to be interchangeable terms. To have the knowledge of good and evil is the mark of the saint, but that saint's disciples frequently suppose that they stand above good and evil, and are freed from the bondage of both.

The second dangerous truth is derived from the plain fact that since evil is a spiritual thing the cure must lie in the sanctification of the human spirit, that henceforth it should live free from sin. It is so easy to forget that sanctification is also a process and not a fact once for all accomplished. To forget it is to be led straight into the second desperate heresy of ethics, that when once the spirit has been sanctified it does not matter what the body does, and " the body can sin without affecting the soul." It was as a protest against this perversion of ecstatic religion that Luther cried out, " Sin lustily that grace may abound." As the religious history of California in the last two hundred years abundantly shows, ecstatic forms of religion are always liable to these two heresies, which completely destroy any grace derived from Christ's life. And yet no religion genuinely worships God unless it has its ecstatic side. The ecstasy of the complete forgetfulness of the self as the heart is lost and found again in the " deep and dazzling darkness " of the Absolute —who has ever known God and not known this?

To say that evil comes from the heart, that it is spiritual in its nature, was thus dangerous, but its danger was the danger always present in truth. A true saying is always a risky saying. This saying carries with it a still further implication. Evil, like good, is spiritual, and is therefore subject to whatever laws govern spiritual growth. Now we are accustomed to speak of beauty, truth, and goodness as a kind of qualitative trinity, and yet that is exactly what they are not. Beauty and truth are both absolutes; they find their perfection in the reposeful contemplation of their own excellence. Spirit, of which both good and evil are manifestations, is different. All spiritual phenomena are possessed by an insatiable restlessness. Conquering one field does but lead them to lay siege to the next. No victory of the spirit is satisfying unless it ensures a further victory still. This is the inherent weakness of evil, that it can never be satisfied; and since every victory spells more and more human suffering, each successive victory is harder to achieve than the last. With good that is not so, for its victories become successively easier.

Evil must grow or perish, and that is the law of its being. It is so because, being spiritual, it is insatiable. It wins one victory only to win another, and if it loses the second it has already reversed the verdict of the first. The supreme example of the law of the growth of spiritual evil is of course Calvary. At the Cross absolute unmixed evil came into conflict with absolute unmixed good for the first and the only time in history. The immediate result was the victory of evil. The devil had his way with Jesus, and whatever good there was in Pilate, the Pharisees and the disciples, was turned to its own confusion and to the service of the devil. This illustrates a principle which must always be recognised by all moral realists : whenever evil comes into conflict with good evil will always win—at first—and this is just as true of politics and economics as of personal morality. Jesus, then, was led away to be crucified and the devil had won his first victory. But that was not enough. It was indeed useless unless it could be promptly followed by a second victory. The devil had beaten His body, but there was no real triumph in that unless he could also beat His spirit. They came to nail Him to the Cross and at once siege was laid to His spirit. Would He deny His teaching and curse His enemies? If He did, the power and the glory would pass to the Evil One. If not, from the Evil One would be taken away even that victory which he already had. Jesus prayed for His enemies and the devil fled shrieking. In that moment the Cross had become the symbol of the defeat of evil for all time, and the devil had himself made it so. He had won the first victory, but in losing the second he was routed by the very victory he had just won.

One difference between the laws governing evil and good thus declares itself. Evil must go "from triumph to triumph advancing," and it cannot survive failure. It lays gradual siege to a man's soul, to a human society, or to a political system, and it wins, very likely, most of the earlier, cheaper victories. But if at any stage it loses a single engagement it loses all. It is as though the earlier victories had never been won. They themselves become instruments of evil's defeat. Evil can feed only on success, and it cannot stand failure. But with good this is not so. It is precisely on failure that good flourishes. It is when a man is humiliated by his constant failure to withstand the assaults of temptation that he is most likely to throw himself upon God's grace and beseech divine help. With that grace he can triumph, but over and over again he would never have asked for it if failure had not taught him the futility of relying on his own strength.

With our limited time-bound minds we may not be able to solve the problem of why evil exists, but we do know that because it exists a greater good is often possible than would have been possible without it. But, granted the common spirituality of both good and evil, it is not possible to reverse the sentence and write, "Because good exists a greater evil is possible than would have been possible without it." Not only, therefore, are the overt acts of good and evil different, but also the deeper laws of their being are different too.

None the less, evil has an initial advantage over good in that it makes the easier and swifter appeal to that which alone governs the human will. "I could be good if I would," said St. Augustine, " but I won't. Who will make me ? " What does govern the human will ? Certainly not the intellect, for the intellect by itself sets nothing in motion. Nor emotion by itself, for emotion is more fluctuating than purposeful. The real governor of the will is imagination. What we call will-power is really imagination-power ; and the prodigies which the undivided will and the single mind of a Napoleon or a Hitler have achieved have been really due to their ability to hold one picture, and only one, steadily before their mind's eye. They gaze and gaze upon it, and their will is summoned and their sinews stiffened. It is not possible to find a much deeper layer in human consciousness than the imagination, for it is a completely spiritual entity, to which both evil and good, by virtue of the spiritual reality which resides in them, are able to make their appeal. But in this, evil has far the easier task. There is always a strong element of disciplined austerity in the pictures which good presents to our imagination, whereas those of evil are swiftly and immediately attractive. The rewards of an evil act are paid at once and on the spot, whereas the transactions of good are generally on a long credit basis. It is the difference between lust and love. Anyone can lust : it is the easiest thing in the world, and its rewards are both pleasurable and immediate. Love, too, presents a haunting image to the imagination ; but love, being a settled disposition of the mind, can give its rewards only to a mind steadily disciplined and purged. So it is also with the difference between power for power's sake, which is evil, and power for service's sake, which is good. Anyone can desire the first, but to desire the second is possible only to a mind already trained to look upon the things that are excellent.

The forces of evil have the power to strike more deeply still as they make their claim upon human allegiance, for it is the teaching of the Bible that a principle of evil lies at the very heart of the universe, and at the very foundation of the human spirit. " Behold the lamb of God which taketh away the sin of the world "—so John the Baptist introduced our Lord. The word is singular and not plural, sin and not sins, for, as the Archbishop of Canterbury says in his commentary :

> There is only one sin, and it is characteristic of the whole world. It is the self-will which prefers " my " way to God's—which puts me in the centre where only God is in place. It pervades the universe. It accounts for the cruelty of the jungle, where each animal follows its own appetite, unheeding and unable to heed any general good. It becomes conscious, and thereby, tenfold more virulent in man. And no individual is responsible for it. It is an " infection of nature," and we cannot cure it. We are not " responsible " for it ; but it sets us at enmity against God : it is the sin of the world.[1]

It is this fact which the Church attempts to explain in the Doctrine of Original Sin. This doctrine, much derided in the past, is now generally agreed to be a calm and lucid statement of the plain fact that in every man there is something to which evil can make its appeal.

[1] *Readings in St. John's Gospel.* Vol. I, p. 24. (Macmillan.)

But this tendency must itself be evil, or temptation could not appeal to it, and, being evil, it stands in need of the grace and forgiveness and redemption of God. This principle of evil is present in everyone, and not least in the baby that is brought for baptism, and that is why it is not unreal to bestow upon the child forgiveness of its sin, even though at that moment it has not committed any overt sins.

The doctrine of Original Sin is thus no more than a recognition in formal theological language of the obvious reality that there is something wrong with the roots of the universe, and with our own roots as part of it. Jesus accepted it in accepting baptism, St. John proclaimed it, and all subsequent New Testament writers build on it. Our own experience of the world in this generation confirms it at every point. This it is which gives evil its chance, and a fruitful use evil makes of it. But none the less evil is not the only quality which men display, for there is also the good, and if any of their acts are good it must follow that the principle of good is set no less deeply in them than the principle of evil. Unless the doctrine of Original Sin is matched by the doctrine of Original Virtue there is no making sense of our human experience. The life of

Christ could have been of no avail whatever if there was not a principle of essential goodness in humanity to which it could appeal; and the fact that His life has proved itself capable of appealing to the imaginations of all races of men at any and every stage of development is a proof of the existence of a principle of good no less deeply rooted in the structure of the universe, and of human life upon it, than the principle of evil. For this reason it is impossible to go all the way with the school of disillusioned prophets of today, who have swung so far away from the old theories of the inevitability of progress as to proclaim that human nature, without Christ, is simply an evil nothingness, totally depraved and no more. Such was not the view of St. Paul, or even of St. Augustine, and has at no period been held by any considerable body of theologians. Nor was it held by Christ Himself, who, in the parable of the Sower, plainly taught that both the ground and the seed were in themselves good and fruitful. Christianity holds a grimly realistic view of evil, and knows that there is absolutely no depth of depravity to which human beings cannot sink. Both possibilities are latent in every child, because every child has deeply imbedded in it the principles of good and evil.

It could not choose the good without God; but if there were no God its choice of evil would not be evidence of total depravity, unless we are to suppose that the conduct of a shark, a crocodile, or a rat is depraved. Apart from God there is neither good nor evil, neither sanctity nor depravity, but simply an all pervading ethical neutrality, and a series of acts without moral significance.

Thus it is that every considerable religion recognises the conflict of good with evil as inherent in the scheme of things and necessary to the being of a developing universe. This intuition the different religions have symbolised in the various myths, for religion, no less than philosophy, has to deal in mystery, and when it comes to explore regions of consciousness where words are no longer capable of describing its discoveries, it falls back on myth as its vehicle of expression, as Plato also did. These religious myths are of all kinds, some of them perverted and absurd like the whole mythology of ancient Babylon, against which the myth of the Garden of Eden in Genesis was a protest and a battle-cry. But all of them have in common the idea of a double conflict fought out both in the heavens and in the world, between God and the devil with his demons, and between their respective followers in the world of time. These two conflicts are interdependent, and so react on each other and continually spill over into each other. Yet they are always thought of as being distinct and each has its separate prize for which the competitors strive. God and the devil compete for the lordship of the universe. The prize they set before their warring disciples in the world is the mastery of the human soul.

The teaching of our Lord accepts the universal intuition which lies behind these myths, purges them of their crudities, and brings them altogether in the myth which He Himself propounded again and again. For Him a myth was a symbol pointing to truth and standing for truth, and therefore true in itself with the same kind of sacramental and symbolical truth that we predicate of the presence of Christ in the elements of the blessed Sacrament. In His teaching too there is this same dual conflict. The power and drive of evil is seen by Him under two forms and symbols. There is " the World " and there is the " Prince of this world." Their purpose may be the same and their work virtually identical, but they constitute two existences, not one existence under two forms. He speaks of them in different ways, almost with different accents. "The World," from which He said so often that He and His disciples had cut themselves free, was the whole series of motives, the impulses to express them, and the organisations to contain them, which are connected with the whole complex system of rewards and penalties, promotions and failures, popularities and fames, powers and possessions. It is in fact, "society organised as apart from God," and if one text more than another delineates its spirit, it is this: "How can ye believe, which receive honour one of another, and seek not the honour that cometh from God only?" (John v. 44). Of such a spirit and attitude to life the ultimate expression is cynicism, and therefore the World, left to itself is not dynamic but passive. Between its citizens and Christ's disciples there is an enmity as Christ so often said, but the World's warfare is a dull, inert, passive pressure, strictly negative in its modes of expression. Left to itself, it would have no hope of winning, because, being fundamentally cynical, it does not express the dynamic power of evil. But plainly, evil is a most dynamic and by no means defeated power (except in so far as it has suffered *potential* defeat on Calvary), and therefore to equate evil with the World would be to play false to the facts of human experience. There must be some malignant power to lead the World—a power which uses worldly people as its instrument—and which is capable of being isolated and distinguished. Thus in the Garden of Eden, the moral slackness of Eve would not have brought " death into the world and all our woe " if it had been left to itself. It was only when the serpent came on to the scene that " man's first disobedience " could have such catastrophic results.

The insight of the author of Genesis in drawing this distinction between Eve, the passive instrument, and the serpent, the dynamic power, of evil is followed throughout the Bible, and in most religious mythologies. It is as though all the masters of the religious life unite to tell us that we shall never take the measure of evil until we learn to think of it as personal, and so capable of making its appeal to the deep springs of personality in ourselves. It is thought of as personal in the same sense that God is personal, as having definite, recognisable characteristics, as He has, as capable of being known by name, as He is. Its power is of the same species as God's, and thus in the Book of Job the devil withstands God face to face, argues with Him, and is given the greater part of his claim on Job. Our Lord emphatically endorsed all this. He gave to the devil various names, Satan, Beelzebub, the Prince of this World, the Power of Darkness. He accepted the fact that it was given to the devil to hurt the earth, and that, being personal, all the resources of single-minded personality were at Satan's disposal. He emphatically believed in a personal devil, and it is hard to see any justification for abandoning that belief. Rather it is true that everything that has happened in the last ten years has vindicated it.

Our Lord saw the finger of Satan in all the disasters which can happen to humanity, but He left His disciples to piece together from His teaching the elements of satanic strategy, which brings about those disasters, except in so far as He ceaselessly pointed out the nature of the connection which bound together Satan and the World. The mythologists of every age have struggled after a greater precision, and their pictures vary enormously. But they all agree in this, that Satan is to be credited with a most remarkable intelligence, and that his fundamental strategy must be to take good and spoil it, rather than to take evil and intensify it. His real stroke is to be taken for a Christ, his failure is to be recognised for a fiend with horns, hoofs, and a tail. Milton has been constantly abused for making his Satan a rather gallant and sympathetic figure (he even credited Lucifer with compassion), but his insights in *Paradise Lost* come nearer to the reality of Satanic strategy than the insights of most other mythologists :

> Whereto with speedy words th' Arch-Fiend reply'd.
> Fall'n Cherub, to be weak is miserable.
> Doing or suffering ; but of this be sure,
> To do ought good never will be our task,
> But ever to do ill our sole delight,
> As being the contrary to his high will
> Whom we resist.   If then his providence
> Out of our evil seek to bring forth good,
> Our labour must be to prevent that end,
> And out of good still to find means of evil ;
> Which oft-times may succeed, so as perhaps
> Shall grieve him, if I fail not, and disturb
> His inmost counsels from their destin'd aim.
>
> (I. 156–168)

Lucifer rightly estimated his chances. Wherever we turn in art or in science, if we penetrate deeply, we come across evidences of this conflict which underlies all things that exist in the space-time world.   The devil cannot hope to win, for fundamentally it is God's world and not his.   But at every turn and point he can challenge God and force a conflict because deep in the structure of the universe, and in the heart of every created thing within it, there lies a principle of evil to which he can appeal. Yet in the challenge and through the suffering he is undone because his rebellion forces on God ever new creative efforts through which His creation is continually being remade at a higher level. Such is the testimony of all the great mythologies, and we are foolish indeed if, misled by our enlightenment, we disregard them all. To master evil we must first understand it, and no understanding seems possible until a place is found in our reading of experience for the devil and his host of evil spirits.

CHAPTER III

SATAN, WHERE IS THY VICTORY?

THE struggle between good and evil is immemorial and from eternity. But, with the exception of the very earliest centuries of Christendom, there is something quite new about the phase which that struggle has reached today. We are facing something more intense, more devoted, more intelligent, and more ably organised than any generation of Christians has faced before. The enmity with which the Church has had to cope in the past has generally been some variant of one of three well-known sources of resentment. The Church has been attacked for being untrue to its Master : as Swinburn said, " I could welcome Christ, if He did not come with His leprous bride, the Church." The theologians have been attacked for spoiling the beautiful simplicity of our Lord's teaching by creeds, dogmas and all kinds of unnecessary elaborations. Christianity has been attacked by sceptics, rationalists and adherents of other religions because they did not believe it to be true. But the hatred of Christianity today cannot be measured under any of these classical headings. For what is being hated now is Jesus Himself for His beauty and His love ; and what is being feared now is precisely Christianity considered as a religion which seeks to make God's love for man known. It is not the explanation it gives of God's love, and not the Church which proclaims it, which are the principal objects of anti-Christ's vehement attention today. What he is doing is to take the love of Jesus and call it degrading, and to take the mercy of Jesus and call it weakness. This is a quite new phase in the struggle of good and evil.

If we ask why all this has happened, why it is that the opposition to Christ has become so vehement in our generation, there are many writers to suggest an answer, for on this subject a considerable library of books has now been written. But they hardly do more than expand and set within the framework of modern circumstances the reason that Jesus Himself gave of this phenomenon. The World hated Him, He said, because He testified of it that its works were evil. Perhaps He had in mind that vivid passage from Wisdom (ii. 11, 12, 14, 15), where the spirit of Evil bestows eloquence on his disciples, and they soliloquise in words exactly applicable to the anti-Christ of 1940 :

> Let our strength be the law of justice ; for that which is feeble is found to be nothing worth. Therefore let us lie in wait for the righteous ; because he is not for our turn and he is clean contrary to our doings : he up-braideth us with our offending the law, and objecteth to our infamy the transgressings of our education. . . . He was made to reprove our thoughts. He is grievous unto us even to behold : for his life is not like other men's, his ways are of another fashion.

Christianity is always offensive in the eyes of the world, therefore, because it has both a moral philosophy, grounded in a supernatural religion and so unshakable, and, when it is necessary, an inconveniently piercing voice. Thus it can testify of the world that its works are evil, and such testimony is deadly because the Church forms its judgments on the only basis from which it is possible to declare the unalterable evil of the characteristic works of the World. In the last analysis these works come to this—the attempt to smash God by reducing the stature of Christ and by denying, in practice and in theory, every-thing that Christ taught about the unique sacred-ness of a man's life. The motive of the World is therefore always the lust for power and its instru-ment is the procreation of tyranny. Only on

Christian pre-suppositions about God and Man can it be said that freedom is always good and tyranny evil. Therefore it is Christianity, and Christianity alone, which is invariably in a position to testify of the World that its works are evil, and for that reason the World is bound to hate the Christian faith.

But when Christendom finds its voice and passes from mute rebuke to eloquent condemnation, Anti-Christ comes on the scene and imbues the fight of the World with an intelligence which it normally lacks and a sort of infernal fieriness which carries it to a good many early and cheap victories. It is probably true to say that we are at war today principally because the Christian condemnation of tyranny has become so vocal and incessant that Anti-Christ must silence it or see the World suffer defeat. The fact that Christianity is hated today with a hatred which has found it unwontedly necessary to go " all out " is really an inverted testimony to the fact that for some years past the Christian warfare against the World has been a good deal more effective than we suppose. Christians on the whole have a poor opinion of the record of the Churches for many years past, and whether that judgment is accurate or not they are right to hold it because it is always good that we should judge our own side with some severity. But the hosts of Anti-Christ at least think sufficiently well of us to fear us and to put all they know into their effort to win this phase of the immemorial conflict.

For this reason Christianity is News with a capital N over most of the earth today. The social outcasts praise Jesus because they believe His teaching leads to a just ordering of society. The refugees praise Him because He is the Prince of Peace. The chronically frustrated praise Him because they see security, the pearl of great price, shining dimly through the pages of the Gospel. The racially dispossessed praise Him because there is no respect of persons before God. All who long for righteousness praise Him because they see in Him the gate leading to the way out of the city of destruction wherein they dwell. Contrariwise, the warmongers, the cunning counsellors, the heartless magnates, and those who are avid for power, curse Him because He rises up in judgment against them and threatens to tear the people out of their clutches. That today for all humanity Christ or Chaos is a true choice is now generally accepted, intellectually by those able to judge and weigh events, devotionally by those trained to maintain their communion with God, instinctively by the plain man who does not pretend to be able to understand these high matters but sees spread before him the hell which has crowned a secularist period of history. That paganism, when built on an apostacy from Christainity, is in actual practice a cruel and beastly thing is plain for all to see. At last there is an end of humbug in political high places and the choice plainly declares itself, righteousness with God or misery with the pagan World.

No wonder Christianity is news today. No wonder it is hated. Christians who look at this hatred with a sense of injured astonishment must be blind. What else did they expect? Certainly our religion is hated and feared, as it always has been and always will be until at last the World itself is redeemed. But today that hatred and fear is more intelligent and forceful than it has ever been since the day when Caiaphas found memorable words to express it. And it is so because Anti-Christ has come again.

Now it must be the purpose of an intelligent as opposed to a stupid devil—and Anti-Christ is most intelligent—to enlist the virtuous in his cause, as well as the depraved, and this he can only do if he can so disguise his cause as to make it seem to be heading towards a righteousness which most men feel they need. Hence the warning always is that the devil will seem to many to be another Christ, and this deception will be no cheap fake, but will work, and lead astray many who sincerely look for the coming of God. But if he is to seem to be God he must work like God; and just as God is revealed by an Incarnation, so the method of the Spirit of evil at moments of decisive conflict seems to be to choose a human instrument to indwell.

At this point, no doubt, most readers will be expecting me to name Adolf Hitler as the incarnation of the devil for our generation. If at least four other names were added to his there might be much justification for this, for clearly the spearhead of the attack on the Christian faith is at present located in Germany, Italy and Russia. There is, of course, a certain truth in such an identification, but only part of the truth, and if we stop there we miss so much of the point that we cannot appreciate the devil's real cleverness nor take the measure of the strategy that he is using. For Anti-Christ is at bottom a system of thought which uses as its mouthpieces not only the people whose sound is gone out into all the world—the great international criminals—but also every other person who approves this system of thought and spreads it. That the devil is incarnate in various men in the world is true ; that he is fully and solely incarnate in any one of them, as God was in Jesus, is not true. We must not look first at Hitler or at Stalin if we would understand. We must ask what line of thought it would be which most swiftly undid the work of Christ, and would at the same time be likely to impose on sincere, kindly people the fallacy that it does but fill up that which was lacking in His work, and carry it by a convenient short cut to its logical conclusion. Wherever we can find and isolate this line of thought we shall find Anti-Christ's work, and then we can start with our identification of his chosen instrument. It may then be that we shall discover with some horror that he has been using ourselves.

Now the essential work of Jesus was, and is, to set men free to be that for which God created men, and, as St. John said, it is by the Truth that they are freed. It therefore follows that the effect of the work of Jesus is to give dignity to humanity. This the Spirit of Evil presumably wishes to reverse, and to reverse it is to drive out of men's hearts even the desire to be free, to make them all enthusiastically consenting slaves. To achieve this is no light matter. It involves the creation of nothing less than a new kind of man, a collective man, who thinks with the herd, feels with the herd, and indeed *is* the herd epitomised. The triumph of economic mass production, with its war on variety of every kind in the goods we consume and the work we do, plainly provides some of the groundwork upon which it is possible hopefully to set oneself to create the Collective Man. But mass production was what the World was stupidly content to rely on before Anti-Christ came to lead it ; and of course it is not enough. The really decisive stroke is to destroy the instrument which Jesus used to set men free, or rather to destroy our power to use it. This can be done in part by giving the very slightest of tilts to a man's sense of that which Jesus desired to strengthen in him, his dignity as a person. For observe the line of Anti-Christian pleading we so constantly hear in Germany and elsewhere, and even in England. It is an attack on our conviction of sinfulness, on the grounds that it is inconsistent with human dignity that we should be always whining about our sins and howling for forgiveness. Dignity, it is said, is virtue. Convince a man that he is virtuous and his dignity takes care of itself. Give him an ideal of conduct which is really very easy, as for example the precept, " That is moral which serves the nation," and his sense of human dignity is already there, won for him by a short cut. There is no longer any need for a living Christ, and that inconvenient Figure, His ambitions of dignity for the human race thus brilliantly and cheaply achieved, can become a safely dead hero in a book. It is all very ingenious and thoroughly persuasive. And every time someone says he has no consciousness of sin a further blow has been struck at human dignity in the name of human dignity.

Here we see how English people, and English Christians too, may be very deeply infected by the war on Christianity, and be serving its enemies unawares. For while Jesus is News with a capital N, He is not the kind of news that He would desire. Multitudes, astray in a friendless universe, desire to be loved by God. Still more, knowing that they live precariously in the city of destruction, desire nothing in the world so much as to serve under His leadership, whom alone they are convinced can lead them out of it. But what they don't want is that which He offers first, His forgiveness, and He can lead only those whom He has first forgiven. Only they can be free, only they dignified.

This matter of human dignity is worth pondering still further. It is not, of course, the pearl of great price, but it is good that a man should value and seek it. If human personality really has the sacredness which Christ attributed to it, then to covet a true dignity is a sign that we are setting the value upon it that He did. At certain times in history it seems to be specially desirable, and one of those times coincided with the advent of Nazism in Germany and the temptation to some equivalent of it in many other countries. For we should all agree that the period from 1918 to 1930 in Europe was not one in which European humanity cut a very dignified figure. There are in fact very few periods in which humanity was more truly the slave of its circumstances ; and the essence of dignity is the mastery of environment. All ordinary men and women of Western Europe felt it bitterly. One tiny symptom, the spontaneous burst of applause which nightly greeted the remark at the end of Noel Coward's *Cavalcade*, when they drink to England's recovery of her ancient dignity again, showed how deeply we felt it. And if we in England were ashamed of being less than human how ashamed was the average German ? At that time, therefore, to appeal to a man's sense

46

of his dignity as a person was to appeal to something which carried the promise of an explosive response. In such circumstances there are two possible appeals to make, one easy and the other difficult. You can say either, " Find your dignity in the service of the State," or " Find it in the service of God." But if you say the latter you have to point out that the road lies through the apparently undignified process of humiliation, contrition, and forgiveness; that is, you must assert human mastery over environment by a contrary assertion of humanity's utter helplessness without God. But the former way has none of these contradictions; it seems a short cut by a much easier road to exactly the same goal. The subtlety of Anti-Christ consisted in this, that he took and proposed a plainly Christian end, but pointed out the means of an attractive short cut. The result is what we know it to be. Those who travel by it become consenting slaves, twenty times more undignified than before, and involved willy-nilly in warfare against Christ, and the whole process is set in motion through a slight but devastating perversion of that in them which is good.

Human dignity is human freedom ; and human freedom is meaningless unless it is freedom to lead the Good Life. That is why we are free or enslaved in proportion as the truth is in us. It is by the truth that we are set free, and the truth about God and Life and man is what Jesus came to reveal. The method of intelligent attack upon human freedom is therefore to destroy a man's sense of truth, and to undermine his loyalty to the concept of " Truth for its own sake and at any cost."

If this is so, we are at last in a position to identify Anti-Christ. He is a stream of thought, incarnate in all who deliberately subscribe to it, and to some degree incarnate in those who subscribe to it without in the least knowing what they do. This stream of thought rises in a doubtfulness about Truth as such, in the sort of mind that Pilate had, and issues in a denial of Truth. That is to say that Anti-Christ is Nihilism, the belief in nothing—nothing whatever. But even " nothing " must take a positive form before it can become an assertion, and in its positive form it is, of course, " Power for its own sake," than which no idea in the world could be more profoundly nihilistic. But observe once more the intelligence with which Christianity is attacked. To a generation resentfully conscious of its powerlessness comes the invitation to win back its dignity by an assertion of power. Is it any wonder that multitudes were led astray, and have become consenting slaves in the effort to destroy in the name of human dignity that which is actually its backbone and its soul, the religion of Jesus Christ? Nihilism is the true enemy wherever it is found, and the particular figures of Hitler and Stalin only in so far as they are more consciously, fully, and deliberately its servants than most people.

But here we are in company with Hitler and Stalin once again, which is unfortunate but perhaps unavoidable, for all roads in the modern world do somehow seem to lead to them. Yet it is unfortunate because I am anxious not to give the impression that they are in themselves Anti-Christ in the flesh, or that they invented the nihilistic weapons they are using. Neither seems of big enough stature to sustain so colossal a part, and the spirit which is directing the attack on Christianity is of heroic stature indeed, for never has the attack assumed forms of such subtelty, such intelligence, and such devotion. Hitler and Stalin, as representing the militant idolatries called by their names, are certainly its spearheads. They have learned exactly how to handle its chief weapon, Nihilism; but they did not invent it, and they did not create the circumstances which gave it its power. They are the creatures, not the lords of their environment. It has them in its toils today, and they are not able to call a halt.

We can only understand them if we ask what made them what they are. What is it that they have inherited and exploited so skilfully? How is it that for the first time in history, Nihilism, the most completely unattractive of all the world's creeds, has attained so great a hold?

The ordinary answer is given in terms of such events as the Versailles Treaty, the Ruhr Occupation, the Economic Crisis, and so on. No doubt all these things were important, but it is absurd to attribute to them alone the Anti-Christian madness which has so much of the world in its grip, and which is the deep cause of this war. For the heart of the crisis is not political at all, and still less economic. It is spiritual. It is a crisis not of the relationships of Britain and Germany, but of Christianity and the new religion of Anti-Christ. And the driving force of Anti-Christ is the attack on Truth, the Nihilism which expresses itself exactly in the slogan Power for Power's Sake, and not in the least in the idea of Power for the Nation's Sake, or the Proletariat's Sake, which is merely a mask. At bottom it is all a question of Truth and a man's response to it. If he responds to it, even though he realises he can never " know " it, he is armoured against the chief weapon of Anti-Christ, and there is always a chance that he will be able to possess his soul in freedom. But if he cannot respond to it then his soul is the seed-ground of Nihilism, and he cannot be free. He cannot respond if he is quite uncertain whether the term " Truth " has either meaning or existence. That is exactly the modern man's trouble. The waters of many streams, each one of which was nicely calculated to shake a man's belief in the possibility of Ultimate Truth, to turn him into a cynical Pilate, have all flown together into a single great river in one genera-tion. These are the waters made ready for Anti-Christ and his nihilistic agents, and they have troubled them to some purpose.

I cannot do much more than give a bare list of these tributory streams, or, to change the metaphor, these precursors of militant Nihilism. (Even Anti-Christ has his equivalent of John the Baptist.) First among them is the fact that the present stage of research in the physical sciences has led to a momentary intellectual chaos and

D 2

confusion. The more the sciences dig down to discover the material reality on which they rest, the more they seem to demonstrate that ultimate material reality does not exist. Science professes to deal with that which can be measured, but today it postulates energy as its basic reality, and energy is immeasurable. Moreover, the anti-social uses to which every scientific discovery can be put, and commonly are put, have done much to destroy the faith which was once almost universal, that science is a benefactor of humanity. And so too with most of the other shibboleths in which we have long been encouraged to put our trust—humanism, or the belief that man could save himself; education, once thought to be the panacea for all ills; industrial technology, supposed to relieve man of his immemorial bondage to monotonous toil but succeeding only in forcing him to go all his days in fear of unemployment; and democracy, which claimed to set him free, but which by its materialism had all but destroyed its power to free him from the tyranny of money.

Virtually every political, social, and intellectual crutch on which we were encouraged to lean has broken. It happened that the inescapable knowledge of these various betrayals came to us all at much the same time, in the decade 1925 to 1935, and then was supplemented by the greatest of all shocks in the awful knowledge that multitudes of quite ordinary people had not even forsaken the primitive love of cruelty. What, apart from God, was there left to believe in? And belief in God was not yet fashionable again. The ground of Western Europe was littered with smashed idols. Only one was still left to fall, nationalism, and that the events of the Spanish Civil War broke. There then seemed nothing whatever left to believe in, and what sort of hold could an abstract concept like Truth then have? Such a situation Anti-Christ inherited. He did not need to do much. There seemed nothing left to believe in. " Very well," said he, " let us put it positively; believe in nothing—nothing whatever." And he added to himself, " That means, though you don't yet know it, that you will have to believe in me."

Thus we are able to identify the psychological and intellectual train of cause and event upon which Anti-Christ is likely to fight successfully, and, with it, perceive the strategy which he must use. He succeeds always to a situation of which the outstanding feature is contradiction and the vital principle is inconsistency. That is why for a decade past Western Europe has yielded itself so completely to be his stamping-ground. For in that period almost all fields of self-expression have been distinguished precisely by interior contradictions. In sociology and economics we have had poverty in the midst of plenty, and nothing could be much more contradictory than that. But it is in politics that the principle of inconsistent contradictions has been most outstanding. There Nihilism has indeed been enthroned. "Non-Intervention in Spain" suggests to most of us the exact opposite of what the phrase means; and, of course, the deliberate and principled inconsistency of all, and not merely German and Russian, totalitarian diplomacy is fresh in all our minds. International politics in the days of the Tudors is not exactly a savoury study, but at least they were not conducted by men who believed in absolutely nothing except power, in itself nihilistic, and most certainly not in any of the slogans which from time to time they might use. No greater mistake could be made than to suppose that this is a nationalistic age. Nationalism has been broken, and mostly by those who never cease to praise it.

But nationalism is still theoretically exalted, and it is in the name of the Patria that Germans and Russians still organise themselves for battle. Their leaders do not believe in it because they believe in nothing, but they have to use it as a cloak and an anodyne. Here again, of course, we come across the contradiction which characterises our age ; just as we do when we see how fatalistic is totalitarian philosophy. They believe in nothing, but they claim to believe in fate, only they call it economic determinism or historical interpretation. It is not for nothing that Christianity has always regarded fatalism as the worst of its enemies. Finally the contradiction shows itself in the actual waging of war, for the most vital of its weapons today is psychological hypnotism.

Modern European politics, in fact, are utterly inconsistent and contradictory ; and it is fast coming to be accepted that this is after all their normal condition. The thing that has led sane men to this pass is their lack of hold on Truth. You cannot impose political untruthfulness as the guiding principle of international relationships upon the mass of the people until Truth, as an idea, means as little to them as it meant to Pilate. To reduce them to that condition of studied agnosticism on the one hand and eager acceptance of fatalism on the other is the primary strategic aim of Anti-Christ.

It would be fascinating to trace the stages by which Europeans have moved from the position when we all believed that there was such a thing as Ultimate Truth, even if we did nothing about it, to the position when we are very dubious about the possibility of Ultimate Truth and would be thankful enough if we could only believe in it strongly enough to enable us to do something about it. One chapter in such a study would have to be given to science with its ethical neutrality, and the picture which, in its present stage of knowledge, it seems to draw of a formless and meaningless universe. Another chapter would be concerned with the psychologists and the impression they so often give of the human mind's hopeless bondage to itself. Another and a far longer chapter would be concerned with the great eighteenth century interpreters of history, and another given to Karl Marx with his theories of Truth as Economic Determinism. But that part of the study is rather academic, and it will be more to our purpose for the moment to look at the position today.

The crucial fact is that Christianity, and all the

higher religions, who hold that Ultimate Truth is a real concept, that it has been revealed in history, and that its outline is knowable to human beings, is faced by a new religion of which the central affirmation is Nihilism—there is no Truth. The bulwarks of it are, of course, in Germany and Russia. In the theory upon which those two nations are living nothing has puzzled the outside world quite so much as this positive enthronement of inconsistency as a living, and even a declared principle of their social life within themselves, and of their relationships with each other and the rest of the world. The story of German-Russian relations is enough to make anyone gasp with amazement, and the story of Hitler's and Stalin's social policy at home is no less astounding. In neither story is there a single point consistent with any other point, nor does there seem to be a single theme for propaganda (such as patriotism) in which either leader has the least personal belief. Their one god is power, and power, of itself, has no connection with truth. Hermann Rauschning has laid us all very heavily in his debt by giving us in his two books, *Germany's Revolution of Destruction* and *Hitler Speaks*, the clue of Nihilism which enables us to make some sort of diagnosis. The works of Nihilism are evil indeed, as we all know, for its logical end is precisely that destruction for its own sake which has in fact turned out to be the guiding idea of both revolutions. The primary difficulty is that when a mind trained to think and speak upon the logic of Ultimate Truth, with its long train of moral ideas which are taken for granted (as, for example, that if you make a promise you must keep it) comes into contact with a Nihilist mind, which believes that truth, if it exists at all, is contingent only, and purely the servant of a man's will, there is simply no ground upon which they can meet. They do not use the same language, and they might as well talk to each other in double-Dutch.

This Nihilism is our enemy in a field far wider than the present war, for there is a sense in which most of us have already caught its first infection. Say in public, for instance, *Magna est veritas et prevalebit*, and watch the look of doubt spread on people's faces. The truth is great, granted; but does it really prevail? Does it prevail, for instance, when it happens to be the truth about a troublesome person whom the state wishes to discredit? It takes some hardihood to say that such a truth prevails in a propagandist age. Jesus was troublesome and was tried and crucified, and that, the Pharisees thought, was the end of Him. Then they found that it wasn't, but there seems to have been astonishingly little attempt to suppress the facts about Him. No one appears to have made the least effort to suppress or hinder the circulation of the Gospels, and the attempts to censor the Apostles' preaching of that Name in the Book of the Acts were only half-hearted. St. Joan was troublesome, and she was put to death after a far fairer trial than most people of her kind ever get. The truth about her prevailed, and no one seems to have doubted that it would. Probably the most disgraceful trial which has ever been held in England was that of Sir Walter Raleigh. The trial of the Earl of Essex was bad enough in all conscience, but, after all, Essex was unquestionably guilty of that with which he was charged. Raleigh was innocent, and everybody, including his judges, knew that he was innocent. The whole conduct of the court which tried him was a scandalous disgrace. The court which tried Van der Lubbe and Dimitrov behaved no worse. We have never come nearer to the Nazi conception of justice than we approached that day. But the truth about Raleigh has prevailed, and not even the most malignant among his judges seems to have doubted that it would prevail or to have taken the necessary steps to prevent it prevailing in the end.

But when we compare the trial of Raleigh with the Treason Trials of a Nihilist State today the differences become clear. Shall we ever know the truth about Martin Niemoller? It is doubtful. It is virtually certain that the truth about Kamenev, Radek, Sokolnikov and the purged Russian Generals will never be known to history. The very purpose of a nihilist state trial is to conceal the truth in the interests of propaganda ; and it is only for this propagandist purpose that a trial is ever held at all. For every troublesome person in a nihilist state who is brought to trial twenty are quietly assassinated without any trial whatever. There were no state trials for any of the victims of the Nazi purge in June, 1934. Perhaps it is significant that more people feel they know the truth about Roehm and von Schleicher who were not tried than about Van der Lubbe and Dimitrov, for whom a great trial was staged.

At first sight it may seem a little disproportionate to illustrate a statement about a concept so vast as Ultimate Truth by pointing to the success of a few modern treason trials. But in fact these treason trials are grimly relevant. They illustrate the extreme difficulty of ever arriving at a particular truth which propaganda desires should be hidden or distorted. They constitute a brand new factor and a very strong one in the forces arrayed against Light and Freedom in the conflict against Darkness and Slavery. There have been many such conflicts in the past, but in them the forces of Light could always reckon on the inevitability of Truth as their chief ally. Can they any more reckon on Truth if the ordinary man has ceased effectively to believe in it? And in the face of a propaganda so triumphant that we can actually watch it destroying all the instruments which in an earlier age would have led to its ultimate undoing, can we wonder if the ordinary man's hold on Truth, as a concept, becomes progressively more shaky?

Happily there are signs of a revolt against this spiritual servitude. All travellers to the United States, for example, testify to the hatred of propaganda felt there by the ordinary citizen; and at the beginning of the war it was tactfully and tacitly agreed by all responsible persons in Britain that we must organise no propaganda in the

U.S.A., but rather leave the truth free to make its own headway there, unassisted by artifice. This is a really hopeful fact. Still more hopeful is the further fact that it has worked. It would seem that the ordinary man, left to himself, has a deep regard for Truth even if the pressure of events and mental climates over many years have shaken his intellectual hold on it.

But we cannot put our trust in the vague belief of the plain man in some Truth of some sort somewhere, or in his brave, but no less vague, theism. These are certainly hopeful facts and a part of the pledge of the ultimate victory of Christianity over its enemies. But they must not blind us to the fact that Anti-Christ stands today in an exceedingly strong position. Strength for him consists in the hold he gets not over those who are knowingly his agents, but over those who are either innocently taken in by him or are driven by circumstances to try to fight him by using his own methods. Now his primary weapon is not war, which is a consequence of his weapon, but the undermining of Truth. War, with all its horrors, is comparatively honest. It is when Truth is so undermined that those who are supposedly fighting against Anti-Christ are bound to make the lie a part of their method and tactic that the genius of the eternal enemy is seen.

Those who most violently repudiate Hitler and Stalin, and are in fact risking their lives to cast them down, are none the less and willy nilly part of the same family as they and share the same history. To some degree they, too, are infected, and they cannot easily escape the infection. For example, the vogue of propaganda is, as I have said, a most potent instrument in the hands of Anti-Christ in his primary effort to drive out of our hearts any sense of loyalty to Truth. But we, who range ourselves on the Christian side of this crusade, cannot avoid being propagandists. Can you defend your conception of what truth is, and what it involves for society, against the utterly unscrupulous propaganda of Anti-Christ, except by indulging in propaganda yourself? And what sort of Truth is it that has to be defended thus? If you resort to propaganda for such a purpose do you not deny the very impartiality of Truth by virtue of which it is worth believing in? Propaganda need not always lie, but it can never be impartial. To some extent we are bound to use the enemy's weapons. No doubt we can say that we use them only to clear the grounds of weeds, but it is no mean stroke on Anti-Christ's part to force his enemies to use his own weapons against him, for, after all, he is likely to be the more expert in their use.

Furthermore, we are all the citizens of a continent in which Anti-Christ has had a good deal of say for the last four hundred years. If his purpose is the enslavement of humanity, in opposition to the freedom of humanity, which is our Lord's purpose, the ground of his victory has not been ill-prepared. The sundering of Europe into separate, competing national states; the separation of economics and sociology from Christian sanctions under the doctrine of *laissez faire*; the raising up of a double standard of public and private morality; and the gradual driving of religion out of the schools, all these, ultimately products of the Reformation, have formed the introduction to a devil's strategy. They do not, either singly or together, constitute that strategy in themselves, for though their results are dire indeed they do not amount to human enslavement because they have not succeeded in creating a new type of humanity, the Collective Man. But they constitute the inescapable preliminary strategy developing over four hundred years, upon which it is possible for Anti-Christ in our own day to launch the final attack upon the citadel of human freedom and personality. Having destroyed, or at least gravely compromised, international subordination to the common good, and the idea that a man must be economically and financially free, he can now go on to set the crown on his effort by destroying the last bastion of the Christian view of man in weaning him from his allegiance to Truth.

This is the heart of our crisis. That is why we are living in days of decision, why our choice is likely to be valid for hundreds of years. We start gravely compromised. We are part of the heritage of four hundred years of weakening Christianity. We are fighting with many of the weapons which Anti-Christ has successfully forced us to use. Yet if we can recover our hold on Truth, we can regain with it all, and more than all, the ground we have lost. For there is this difference between Jesus and Anti-Christ, and between their respective followers. It is through failure that Jesus comes to His kingdom, and it is in weakness that we are made strong. Anti-Christ has many powers, but one he lacks, the power to turn defeat into victory.

This chapter began by asking the question, " Satan, where is thy victory ? " We are now in a position to answer it, though to find the answer we have had to devote our attention more to matters of public policy than of the individual soul. The distinction is in any case unreal. The purpose of the Evil one is to corrupt the soul, and he triumphs as soon as the corruption has gone sufficiently deep to make the soul no longer able to distinguish good from evil. His primary strategy is therefore to attack the idea of Truth in all its citadels, intellectual, spiritual and moral. Truth is dethroned wherever it is no longer held in reverence for its own sake, but is regarded only pragmatically. The moral consequence of substituting pragmatism for Truth is an immediate chaos in ethical terms, whereby we are led to take a plainly bad thing and call it good because we sympathise with the people who did it, or because it seems to help the cause we have at heart ; or, contrariwise, to call a plainly good thing bad because we disapprove of the people who did it and the cause they were serving. In ethics this is the sin against the Holy Ghost, as Jesus Himself said, and for those who habitually commit it there is really little hope. They have mutilated themselves by cutting away the whole moral content of their nature, for once good and evil are regarded as contingent there is no ground left on which good can stand. Then all is evil, because evil has completely mastered the field. How near we in Europe have come to this dreadful abyss can be seen by anyone who will call to mind the history of European partisanship in the Spanish civil war. In that war many foul things were done, but not one was too foul to escape applause from the onlooking partisans of either Right or Left. Every evil act, the murder of priests and the massacre of Guernica alike, found some to call it good ; and throughout there was an almost complete suspension of any standard of ethics on the part of the partisan onlooker. The devil has never stood nearer to his triumph in Europe than he stood then.

Intellectual and political chaos breed the collective mind which cannot know its need of Christ, and chaos in those fields derives immediately from chaos in ethics. Yet this chaos, too, is derivatory and not primary. For ethics, as the Stoics found, cannot stand by themselves. They must be built into and upon a supernatural and spiritual view of the universe. Half our moral troubles, and with them our social and political troubles, come of our forgetting that right and wrong are expressions of good and evil, and that good and evil are spiritual in their nature, built into the heart of a spiritual universe. Irreligious

67

and secular ethics have nothing on which they can stand and are the opportunity of the devil. They lead straight to the nihilistic denial of Truth, and that in turn leads to the undoing of the work of Christ both for society and for man.

CHAPTER IV

THE ETHICS OF TRAGEDY

MOST of the great souls for whom life is a riddle that will not let them alone, but imperiously demands from them an effort of interpretation, and can get no help from religion, are driven back upon tragedy as their interpreting principle. They are not willing to wear the mantle of cynicism or frivolity as they look at life. If they were they would have no greatness in them. They demand that life should make some sort of sense. Their austere irreligion forbids them to hope to find a cosmic meaning, but at least they can look hopefully for an ethical meaning. For them, no less than for those whose minds move more easily among religious concepts, evil is a fact, and this fact must be explained, mastered, and purged before they can offer any coherent explanation of the meaning of life. If they cannot believe that God takes away the sin of the world, tragedy is the only rock left to them on which they can stand. Tragedy is truly a rock, not a delusion. It does offer a coherent answer to the double challenge of evil and good. It does provide a view of life which is both ethical and consistent. Its tradition is therefore as old as the tradition of religion itself. Any account, even a religiously inspired account, of the conflict of evil with good which has nothing to say about the contribution of classical tragedy to the problem stands self-condemned. It would be to take no notice of the witness of half of humanity.

Tragedy is an art-form. It has its rules, but the great artists who have made it what it is have generally left it to the commentators to explain what its rules are. Nor are these rules mere matters of literary convenience. A comedy, or, in music, a sonata, can exist on the general principle of art for art's sake. But a tragedy cannot for its principle is art for life's sake. Its rules are developed accordingly, and are those most calculated to throw light upon the purpose it sets itself, that is, the interpretation of life. A comedy or a sonnet has its rules, but they are not really binding because the beatitude of the comedy or the sonnet is the contemplation of itself as a thing of beauty and a joy for ever. Hence, in these arts any rule may be broken if the breaking of it makes the perfection of beauty and form more easy to portray. But the rules of a tragedy may not be broken. If they are, it is not a tragedy but something else. They may not be broken because the beatitude of tragedy is not the contemplation of itself, but the contemplation of life as a developing process by which evil is purged. To tamper with the rules is to tamper also with essential coherence of the interpretation of life which tragedy provides. Shakespeare more than any others has declared what these rules are, and it is Shakespearian tragedy which is mainly considered in this chapter. Chiefly this is because Shakespeare is the most familiar tragedian to English-speaking people, and most of them are familiar with at least the outlines of plays like *Macbeth* and *King Lear*. But there is another reason. In Shakespeare the human race reached a certain finality in this particular field of its self expression. It is possible that a greater tragic dramatist than Shakespeare may one day be born, though it is most unlikely. But it seems quite impossible that anyone could now be born who could do again, and better, the particular thing that he did. In him, the classical, poetic, dramatic tragedy came to its final fulfilment. When he died there was nothing left to say which could be said in that way. To take Shakespeare as our guide means, of course, that we accept the statement that he was not a religious man, and that, whatever his belief in God may have been—if he had any—at any rate it was not a Christian belief. To say this is to venture on very troubled waters, but the problem of Shakespeare's religious beliefs is so thorny and so complicated, that I must content myself with merely showing this awareness of its complication. What is certainly true is that if the real soul of Shakespeare is disclosed in his tragedies with completeness and without reserve, then his soul was great far beyond our power to measure, but it was not Christian.

If the preceding argument about the rules of tragedy is sound it ought to follow that any exposition of the principles and form of tragedy, as Shakespeare practised it, constitutes in itself a statement of the outlines of the tragic view of life, and its ethical content. But it is necessary first of all to be clear about what tragedy is *not*, for there is hardly any word in the language so constantly misused in common speech. It is not enough for a story to be sad. It is not even enough for its atmosphere to be pitiful and its author charged with the spirit of pity, not even though Anatole France himself declared that pity is the deepest spring of all true genius, for all genius is not tragic genius. If sadness and pity made tragedy then Dickens' *Oliver Twist* might be one of the great tragedies. Yet no one would suggest that it is, nor yet that Dickens had any particle of an aptitude for tragedy. More often than not a tragedy ends in bloodshed, but violent death does not make a tragedy. If it did, any Edgar Wallace thriller might be a tragedy, made so by the sheer weight of the corpses with which he litters his stage. It is true that Edgar Wallace did once come within measurable distance of writing a tragedy, in *On the Spot*, but manifestly he did not speak the language, breathe the air, or think the thoughts of Shakespeare.

But sadness and pity are always, and blood is usually, present in a tragedy. What makes them tragic is how they come, and what light they cast on the souls that give them. The blood comes because to shed it is usually part and parcel of a conflict. The sadness and the pity are there because this conflict is not the simple collision of good with evil but of good with good, or, to speak more accurately, of one kind of good with another kind of good. That is pitiful from the ordinary earthly point of view. From the more detached and serene point of view it is still more pitiful, for besides the breaking of human souls there is the agonising sense of utter waste. To get the full savour of a tragedy, therefore, the reader, or spectator, must himself be conjured into the illusion of this serene detachment. He is to look on horrors, but must not be merely horrified. He is to be swept by pity, but must find that pity purging and exalting. He must be overwhelmed in sadness and yet be led to exclaim, " How great a thing is man." This he cannot be if, as he watches, he has the impression that the characters are just like himself, that they are, so to speak, Tom, Dick and Harry dressed up, and speaking his own thoughts in archaic language. Many true tragedies are unfolded every day in the police court, but they have not the value of tragedy for those who listen to them there. Tragedy is so mighty a thing that only the very greatest souls are capable of sustaining a tragic part without looking slightly ridiculous. Therefore a theme may be the conflict of good and good, involving waste, and still not be truly tragic. To become that it must be worked out with characters of heroic stature. This last principle has an important inference. It is that tragedy requires for its unfolding not merely an author and actors, a story and a stage, but also an audience or a body of readers. Comedy would still be comedy if the theatre was empty, but tragedy would no longer be itself. Tragedy, besides being an art, is ethical and purposive. It sets out an interpretation of life. It shows the world to the world. It needs to be looked at, and those who look help to make it what it is. They are as essential to it as a body of worshippers is to the Mass. Just as fidgety, talkative, and inattentive worshippers can wreck any Mass by depriving it of something essential, even though their behaviour would not make any difference to the reality of the Consecration, so an audience which refuses to enter into the spirit of a tragedy can reduce it to the level of a blood-and-thunder drama.

To say that tragedy is the conflict of one kind of good with another is to assert the diversity of goodness. In *Macbeth*, for instance, the conflict is provided by the ambitions of Macbeth and Lady Macbeth who are profoundly wicked. But in their very wickedness they are great. The ambition that consumes them burns them like a fire and sets blazing all they see. But it is an infirmity of profoundly noble mind, in which the greatness and nobility has gone wrong. Othello was no doubt a jealous husband. Had he not been so the malignant whispers of Iago could not have had so dreadful a result. But his jealousy was the fruit of an intensity of love so devoted that ordinary people cannot hope to share it. In *Hamlet* the conflict is internal, not external. It is fought out in the hero's soul. Yet there, too, it is precisely his sensitiveness which causes all the trouble, and is responsible for the wreckage of a sudden, untimely end to seven lives. In *Antony and Cleopatra*, too, it is Cleopatra's very greatness, her "immortal longings," brought into conflict with her love for Antony, that cracked a noble heart.

There is no need to take all the Shakespearian tragedies one by one to show that they are built on the conflict of good with good.

What is more important for our present purpose is to notice an inference which arises from it and which illustrates the nature of the ethical system which tragedy sustains. Tragedy ends always with an overwhelming sense of infinite sadness and frustration, and this misery is caused by the very virtues of the hero. In *King Lear*, for instance, all hell is let loose, but who loosed it? It was the noble Cordelia, and she was led to do so by the very passion of integrity which was her strength. Her sister

Goneril fulsomely protested a love for their father she never felt :

> Sir, I love you more than words can wield the matter.
> Deeper than eye-sight, space, and liberty,
> Beyond what can be valued, rich or rare
> No less than life : with grace, health, beauty, honour,
> As much as child e'er loved, or father found,
> A love that makes breath poor and speech unable.

But not her speech, nor Regan's either, which abounded no less in " that glib and oily art," loosed the storm. When Cordelia's turn came, her integrity, her impotence to speak an insincere word though her life hung on it, held her dumb. She had

> a tardiness in nature
> Which often leaves the history unspoke
> That it intends to do.

So she could say no more than her heart bade her, and that was too little.

> I cannot heave
> My heart into my mouth : I love your majesty
> According to my bond, nor more nor less.

Her life, her happiness, her wealth hung on her speech ; and not her life only, but the lives of so many others too. Her strength was her complete integrity, on any showing and in any setting, a quality of high moral worth. But it was her weakness too. Provoked by her sisters' oily arts, she could not even touch the old man's hand. By the weakness that came of her very strength the storm was loosed.

In *King Lear* the conflict is over in the first scene and the rest of the action shows its consequences. In *Hamlet* the conflict in the hero's soul is only resolved in death and we watch its slow unfolding. In the other tragedies the conflict is more external. But, however it is staged and managed, the end is always the same, the wasteful ruin of the good. The evil is purged but the cost is enormous. The good must perish to purge it, and at the end the stage is left populated by such a collection of mediocrities that we ask whether any purpose can really be ethical which has to be served by so great a waste and ruin. The world of tragedy is neither optimistic nor pessimistic, for tragedy is beyond either optimism or pessimism. But it is profoundly gloomy and yet the gloom is not absolute. "The rest is silence," says the dying Hamlet, and there is just this very faintest of hints that the last words about life in the world have not yet been said. The Archbishop of Canterbury, in the chapter on

"The Meaning of Tragedy" in *Mens Creatrix*, estimates the weight to be given to this faint hint :

Hamlet breaks off his last speech to murmur "The rest is silence," but Horatio does not accept that :

Now cracks a noble heart. Good-night, sweet Prince,
And flights of angels sing thee to thy rest.

No doubt Horatio is a commonplace sane person, who might be expected to believe in immortality ; but the fact that Shakespeare put the words into the mouth of a suitable person is no evidence that he regarded them as unimportant. Of course this passage does not prove Shakespeare's belief in immortality, or even suggest it ; my point is that the occurrence of these words colours the whole conclusion of the play—as with the faintest touch of light in the utter gloom, a glimmer that may be the herald of a new dawn. Professor Bradley suggests that this may be permitted here by Shakespeare because Hamlet alone of all the heroes is in gloom from the very opening of the play. I should feel this argument more strongly in the case of the similar passage in *King Lear*. After the King is dead, Albany invites Kent to take a share in the government of the kingdom, and Kent replies :

I have a journey, sir, shortly to go ;
My master calls me, I must not say No.

Surely this is more than a mere refusal to survive his master, which is all that Professor Bradley sees in the lines ; I am clear that to me at any rate the lines have an immense value—not that the light that they bring into the gloom is bright, for it is barely discernible, but they make all the difference between total and just not total darkness.[1]

[1] *Mens Creatrix*. William Temple. Pp. 147, 148. (Macmillan.)

But the sense of waste and gloom, and the despairing cry, What sort of a world is this ?—these are the pre-occupations of the mind lying awake in bed hours after the play has been seen and he has left the theatre. But while the whole being of the spectator is swept by its sway, his impressions are different. His first sense is that he is being made aware once more of the greatness of man. Men and women may come to a dreadful end, being led thereto so often by that which is best in them, but at least they are not small if they can endure so much and yet hope. From this realisation that, put things at their worst, and paint the blackest picture that the facts warrant of life, man emerges profoundly great in his own right, and in his capacity to endure, comes the sense of an exhilarating exaltation. Waste, yes ; ruin, yes ; gloom, yes ; and yet somehow this most disinterested of all testimonies to the worth of man makes it all worth while. Whatever tragedy is, it is never an argument for suicide. Nor does it paint the picture of a life that is purposeless, for in the process the evil does get purged and overcome and that is life's purpose. Iago and Macbeth are killed, and the self-seeking Goneril and Regan are exposed. So the life it portrays has a purpose and is not aimless. It is evidence of Shakespeare's belief in the brave austerity of the natural man's soul that he trusts his audiences and his readers to see it.

Nobility is thus inherent in the very stuff of tragedy. It takes life as its raw material. It tacitly denies the divine governance of life. It dismisses any redemptive action other than such redemption as men themselves can bring about. That is to say, it is tacitly dismissed in tragedy, but tragic authors are not necessarily tragedians all the time. Elsewhere Shakespeare explicitly affirms the divine redemption, as, for instance, when Isabella pleads for Lucio in *Measure for Measure* :

> Why, all the souls that were were forfeit once :
> And He that might the vantage best have took
> Found out the remedy.   How would you be
> If He, which is the top of judgement, should
> But judge you as you are ?

But *Measure for Measure* is not a tragedy. It is not in his comedies or in his chronicle plays that Shakespeare faces resolutely every grim fact which life holds, but in his tragedies. And out of this profoundly unpromising raw material tragedy weaves a picture, dark and agonising indeed, but both purposive and ethical. It paints a developing, not a static universe, though the motion of its development is cyclic. It holds firmly the utter hostility and unlikeness of good and evil, and it interprets the purpose of life as the purging of the evil. It points to man as a being of magnificence and glory. The devil is not entitled to a crumb of consolation from any who hold the tragic view of life, for tragedy shows evil as always involved in self-destruction by the sheer necessity of its own negations. It says the utmost that can be said for a world in which ethics is not built on a supernatural foundation, and mediated through an incarnation of God. Tragedy is the limit of nobility to which development of stoical, self-sufficient ethics can come.

But it denies human free-will. No doubt it is theoretically true that Hamlet could have refused to accept his cursed destiny to set right the times that were out of joint. But he could only have refused it by ceasing to be Hamlet. The possibility of conversion is at no point envisaged. Even when he posed a deliberate choice to himself in his soliloquy, " To be or not to be," we feel that it was simply a piece of self-justification, and that he was not free to refuse the choice which destiny had already made for him. Tragedy is bound to belittle humanity at this single, but fatal point in the interests of the one deity it acknowledges. For it is not atheistic. It acknowledges a divine creation but not a divine governance of the world. Its God is destiny and its religion fatalism. Its heroes are in no sense free because they are fated. They struggle against their fate, but their struggle is vain from the start. Over all the action broods an inexorable fate. The fate is neither malignant nor benevolent. It is simply unheeding. The famous protest, " Like flies are we to the gods ; they kill us for their sport," is not typical of the religion of tragedy. The tragic gods do not find either sport or pity in their contemplation of human affairs. They are those who made the rules of the game of life, weighted them heavily against any who hope for happiness from living, and then have turned their eyes away. These gods remain eternally unaware of the worship offered to them, unmoved by our fervent prayers, indifferent to our abuse when we blaspheme against them. Everything is destined, and in the world of tragedy there is only fate. Man continually rebels against it because he is created with that incurable discontent which always spells his ruin but is also the condition of his development. This rebellion turns out badly for the particular rebel, but ensures the existence of a developing

F 2

universe in motion. The tragic gods of fatalism have so set the stage that their purpose must infallibly be done, and the agents of that purpose infallibly be brought to utter frustration and ruin. Yet these agents are great even in their ruin, and in the world of tragedy men are better than gods.

CHAPTER V

THE TRAGIC DRAMA OF TODAY

THE contemplation of Shakespearian tragedy is neither academic nor irrelevant to the theme of this book. If we are to master the evil of 1940 we must understand the theory of evil, which in its essence is the same in every generation, and Shakespeare's thought ranged so wide and pierced so deep that it is as germane in 1940 as it was in 1603. The scale has become vaster with the passing years but the principles are still the same. There is, moreover, a considerable school of thought, to be chiefly found among the younger theologians and the representatives of the Christian student world, which is convinced that the only way of hopefully presenting Christianity today is to present it as God's answer to tragedy. In other words, they are convinced that there are only two noble interpretations of life ; the one is the interpretation of tragedy and the other is the interpretation of the Cross of Christ. There is so much to be said for this view that many people will agree that they are certainly right. Experience with many types of congregations, ranging from great cathedrals to the most remote country hamlets, shows that a sermon having this for its theme invariably wins a close attention and provokes spontaneous discussion.

To the citizen of 1940 the word Evil at once suggests the totalitarian system of government. It means concentration camps, official torturers, the glorification of war, lying diplomacy, the persecution of the Jews, the systematic perversion of youth, and the attack on freedom. As these things have led half a world into war once more, and have already involved the ruin and starvation of whole nations ; and as we in England and the British Empire have been chosen, with all our sins, to stand alone to defend the view of life which condemns these things as wrong, it is inevitable that such facts as those should dictate the terms of the current ethical problem we all have to solve. Not only is this identification inevitable, but it is also right. If the totalitarian system, as exemplified in the foreign and domestic policies of Germany, Italy, Russia and Japan, is not evil, in a singularly concentrated and disgusting form, there is no meaning in language. The fact that this vast and organised evil is but the selfishnesses, the complacencies and the faithlessness of multitudes of ordinary people, both among us and among them, writ large, does but add point to the identification. If ever the devil was at work in the world, he is at work in it today, and no contemporary theory of ethics can possibly get far away from the ethical breakdown of Europe, which is the primary cause of the war.

We must, therefore, look for a moral principle by which to interpret the conflict, and we find that the categories of tragedy contain it with an almost uncanny precision. Tragedy is the conflict of one form of good with another. This conflict is between democracy and totalitarianism. Democracy is good in itself. Its theory is Christian at every point. Its destiny of development is the Kingdom of God of which Jesus spoke. There is absolutely nothing in its theory which is not good, and in consequence its betrayal from within produces perversions which are simply devastating. Yet these perversions are not democracy. They are simply a caricature. Totalitarianism is evil if the Christian view of life is accepted. But it is not simply a conflict of good with evil, because totalitarianism has done much incidental good. And even if as a system it were as sincerely evil as its leaders are sincerely evil considered as men, that evil has deep elements of greatness in it. It is not meanly evil, like the sneak thief or the habitual adulterer. Its evil is on the grand scale, the product of a mind which at least is not petty. Between Hitler and Macbeth there are many parallels. Thus the second principle of true tragedy is also fulfilled in the present war. The conflict is worked out in characters of heroic stature. This is so, however one chooses to interpret the word Characters. If it is a conflict between Hitler, as the incarnation of the totalitarian revolution, and Winston Churchill, the incarnation of Western democracy, as American wireless commentators like to define it, then both are characters of heroic stature. Their respective conceptions of greatness are no doubt worlds apart, but within the limits of those conceptions both are great. If one changes the names of the contestants to Good and Evil, Slavery and Freedom, Despair and Hope, Paganism and Christianity, or any other pair of opposites, the same is true. This war is unquestionably a conflict of one sort of good with another sort of good, worked out in characters of heroic stature. Its end, too, is the purging of evil by the sacrifice of the good, and so it involves waste so staggering that it is beyond the capacity of the mind to compute it. To get rid of Iago,

Othello and Desdemona had to die. What is going to be the price of getting rid of Hitler and all he stands for? Has Europe to be destroyed to purge this evil? If tragedy really contains the only clue to interpret our human experience, there is not much doubt about the answer.

That it does not contain this clue, but has passed into something wiser and more embracing than itself it is the purpose of these pages to argue. But first we must pause to notice another most significant attribute of tragedy which is being faithfully reproduced in our own world. This is its religion of fatalism—the only religion known both to tragedy and to totalitarianism.

The word Destiny is one of the key words to unlock the door to the understanding of modern history. No single word plays a greater part in our contemporary world, and it is one of our major disasters that a word which should suggest thoughts of serenity and resignation is everywhere being used to cloak brutality and to further war. Yet we should not be surprised, for this was what the word suggested to Shakespeare. When Italy was earning the moral condemnation of the world by invading Abyssinia she protested that she did but fulfil her destiny and could plainly do no other. Germany has consistently used the same plea and uses it still. There is no horror she has not committed, both against her own people and against others, but her conduct in this, as in all else, is righteous, for she does but walk down the path which history has marked out for her. In the mouth of her leaders, the phrase Racial Destiny has become virtually a synonym for the effort totally to annihilate first the Jews and then the Poles. Similarly, when a Japanese diplomat finds it necessary to cast a cloak of respectability over the conduct of the Japanese militarists, he almost invariably says that Japan invades China in fulfilment of her destiny. He is, moreover, perfectly sincere in believing that the weight of this plea is sufficient to overturn the charges of the Western moralists. To him it is no humbug. How is Japan to be justly blamed for merely seeking to fulfil the destiny of leading all Asia, if not the whole world, if this is the office which the inexorable fates have appointed for her? If others choose to resist, theirs is the blame. Karl Marx is also full of such teachings. The working class is the destined rising class, as the capitalist class is destined to fall. If the pursuit of this destiny involves the use of weapons of cruelty and fraud against the enemies of the revolution, it is the capitalists, the imperialists, or the Finns who are to be blamed. Their condemnation consists in this—that they have so misread history as not to perceive the fate it has pronounced on them and their like.

The sinister associations with which time has thus surrounded the word Destiny shed a new light on the vehemence with which Christianity has always repudiated every fatalistic explanation of the riddles of life. Destiny, as the totalitarians regard it, is only Fatalism under another name, and Fatalism is as much of an explosive as an anodyne. Dictatorship needs both qualities : an anodyne to drug into a stupor the questing mind and the critical spirit, and an explosive to cause its people to spend themselves in a fine, idealist frenzy without any let or hindrance of moral dubieties. The idea of the historical destiny fulfils both needs. The scruples of those who by nature are decent and kindly, when they are ordered to do some utterly disgraceful duty, can best be laid to rest if they can be transferred on to the back of some impersonal and imponderable force. The historical destiny of the class, the race, or the nation is that force. It is so easy to put the blame on history, and one can be certain that history will never answer back. By a piece of inverted reasoning it is even possible to argue that such a mental process is a testimony to the reality and force of moral principles. To invade Norway, to bomb Rotterdam, to shell Almeria— it is quite possible to refrain from saying that these acts are morally right, even to regret them as morally wrong, and still to be quite sure that they will be enthusiastically done, provided that the idea of destiny is provided as a moral scape-goat. Such language may sound cloudy, but it describes a grim and practical reality. How else can we account for the hideous things which are being done day by day by quite ordinary and decent young people?

Destiny is the dialectical line which history lays down. To misread history, to make a false analysis of its facts—this is the real evil, the only evil a man need worry about, for this is the sin against tragic fatalism for which there is no for-giveness. Trotsky, not Winston Churchill or President Roosevelt, is, or was, public enemy number one in Russia, for this is his crime. Many, none the less, are found to take in hand the dangerous task of interpreting history and eluci-dating national and class destinies therefrom. A demand always begets a supply : it is as true of academic philosophers as economic commodities.

The demand of the newer nationalisms for interpreters of history is both urgent and steady.
Hardly ever before has the interpreter of history
enjoyed such a heyday. Never has his calling
been held in such high honour. He is at once
both the prophet and the priest of the dictatorships. He charts their course, he marks their
bounds, and he is in a very real sense the guardian
of their morals. "That is moral which serves the
destiny of the working class"—or the nation.
The phrase may make us shudder. That it does
not make the subject of a dictatorship shudder is
due to the fact that the interpreter of history, the
Court Astrologer of the twentieth century, has
himself made it inevitable, and made of history
the scapegoat to take upon its shoulders the sins
of us all. The vital quality to be sought in
aspirants to the office of historical interpreter-in-
ordinary is faith. A deep knowledge of history
is quite secondary, and in fact is quite seldom
found. But dictatorships live on faith precisely
because they are fundamentally religious move-
ments, and they demand of their historical interpreters not only that they should themselves be
men of faith, but also that they should be able to
create it in others. "A miracle is an event which
creates faith," said Bernard Shaw in a famous

aphorism. So it may be, but as we have learned to our cost, faith does not need a miracle to create it. A faith in a destiny, entertained in such a universal passion of blind, sacrificial enthusiasm as to invest it with the driving force of Leviathan, can be sustained and, in a sense, created by an event so unmiraculous and pedestrian as the research of a shabby old man with white whiskers in the British Museum, or the effort of a thoroughly obscure university professor in Vienna to explain why Austria had come to the horrible miseries of 1919, and what could be done about it. Neither Karl Marx nor Othmar Spann looked anything more than thoroughly academic historical philosophers, and that indeed is what they were. But they had the gift of creating faith, or proposing a class or national destiny which could be popularised. More than any other pair of men they have created the mental climate of the world in which we have to live. And so with all the other academic interpreters of history, whose works are accounted as inspired by one dictatorship or another. Klages, Rosenberg, Houston Stewart Chamberlain and Sorel were all portents which created faith. That most of us neither admit nor approve what the academic philosophers make of it all does not in the least deny that they are men possessing a faith so strong as to engender faith in others.

The Christian who thinks is likely to be a rather puzzled observer of these phenomena. Undeniably they constitute the logical outcome of fatalism, and therefore of the purely tragic view of life upon which fatalism is sustained. But the more he abhors the practical results of this yielding to the idea of historical destiny the more is he bound to recognise that these ideas at least resemble his own. He, too, lives in a destined world and traces the outlines of this destiny from his venture of interpreting history. He believes that this world is fore-ordained to be the scene and history the record of God's triumph over evil. Thus, like the Marxist and the Fascist, he has that which keeps him serenely confident at times when his idea of righteousness seems everywhere in defeat. God is not mocked and His will is eventually done.

Yet there are of course vital differences. It is true that the Christian is as much concerned with the interpretation of history as the philosophers of the new authoritarian paganism, and true again that he approaches his task with a set of preconceived ideas which are at least related to theirs. But, of course, he gets out of history a theory of life which is different. To the authoritarian, destiny is a fate to be worked out in full cycle, not only within the limits of the space-time world, but also within the limits of foreseeable time. The Christian, on the other hand, proposes for the world a final destiny which is tied both to the human vision of God and to the ideal of affording to God the ultimate creative satisfaction of rejoicing in the perfecting of the world which He made. In the nature of things that destiny can never be totally fulfilled within the limits of the space-time world. The ultimate goal of progress is, therefore, transferred to the realm of eternal verities, and it is precisely what the Christian makes of history that transfers it there.

Similarly, to the Christian, that is a true interpretation of history which tends most toward the liberating of most men and a false interpretation which tends to enslave them. History for the Christian turns upon a single pivot, the life, death and resurrection of Christ, an event taking place itself within the historical scheme of things. That event can have no meaning unless a part of it is what the great philosopher, Berdyaev, disclosed, that God does not merely endow men with freedom, but goes further and actually demands freedom from them at every stage of their discipleship. The theory of history in which the life of Jesus Christ is seen to be crucial and pivotal is one which can only be denied and distorted by an effort to cramp human freedom and to stifle human personality. These are vital differences indeed, and they place the Christian and the totalitarian philosophers of history on two sides of a sharp line of division. The fact that they may show certain traits in common and start together from the idea of destiny does not blur that line of division. It is absolute and fundamental, and between the two there can be no accommodation.

But, as the statesmen used never to be tired of telling us, some means of accommodation must be found. They do not tell it to us now, but it is still true. The rival philosophers are fundamentally opposed. What of the historians proper, of whom nothing has yet been said? Those who draw out of history a fate or a destiny are, for the most part, men like Rosenberg and Karl Marx, while the Christian interpreters were yesterday men like St. Paul and St. Augustine, a little later Calvin, and today Nicholas Berdyaev. None of these are historians proper; they are all either philosophers or theologians, who have had to learn some history in order to provide themselves with the raw material of their proper study. The historians themselves, however, are apt to keep silence about the meaning of their craft. One of the most distinguished is, in fact, quite despairing. Professor H. A. L. Fisher began his great work, the three-volume *History of Europe*, with the remark, " Many wiser and more learned than I have discovered in history a plot, a rhythm, a pre-determined pattern: these harmonies are con-cealed from me "; in other words, here is a great historian proclaiming that historical inter-pretation can never be more than guesswork. Happily few historians are so despairing. But the testimony of Professor C. H. Williams' recent anthology of the work of modern historians, called *Modern Historians*, tells much the same tale. Few have stepped aside from their narrative to speculate on what that narrative means. They seem to interpret their task as a duty to tell a story, to say what things happened and how, why and when. It is but rarely that they set themselves the further and still more interesting question, " What do these happenings together mean for human life ? " The historians Professor Williams levies under contribution do, indeed, discuss the technique of their trade, but when they do so they are for the most part contented to argue as to whether history is a science or an art, to defend or attack the increasing fashion of spending one's whole life in illuminating a minute corner of the whole historical field. They are seen using moral or political insights as a means of getting their material in order, and as a principle of selection from the mass of facts which their industry had unearthed. Lord Acton, to whom all historians readily pay tribute, uses his moral insight for that purpose : " I exhort you never to debase the moral currency or to lower the standards of rectitude, but to try events by the final maxims that govern your own lives and to suffer no man and no cause to escape the undying penalty which history has the power to inflict upon wrong." This thought we may couple with his famous aphorism, which every day's newspaper makes increasingly plain, " Power Corrupts, Absolute Power Corrupts Absolutely." That is to use a moral insight as a principle of selection. His predecessor in the Chair of History at Cambridge, Sir John Seeley, used a political insight for the same purpose. To him history was a complicated story which concealed at its heart one plot and one climax, the preparing of the ground for the British Empire and the imperial achievement of Britain. There are, naturally, many exceptions, but the main impression one gets from reading Professor Williams' anthology is that historians as a body have rather rigidly confined themselves to their proper business, the assembling and weighing of evidence and the telling of a tale. But the academic philosophers use history as a means of explaining the trend of life in general and of indicating the kind of goals to which life is moving. They regard the historians proper as their servants and, as we have seen, they get out of the same set of facts a variety of goals, destinies and fates which are quite bewildering.

This is really an *impasse*. It is the riddle of destiny which we are examining. The authoritarian use of the term is seen to lead in practice to all kinds of fraud, violence and cruelty. The Christian use of the term is believed to lead away from them, but is always open to the charge of an utterly uninfluential vagueness, and rests its authority upon a miraculous fact in history which it needs faith to accept. The two views, dispassionately judged, cancel out. The professional historians do not help us to come to a decision about this crucial question of destiny. They present us with our raw materials and tell us to go and think it out again. If we are to escape from the dilemma, we find some new approach.

The new approach is through Professor Arnold Toynbee's masterpiece, *The Study of History*. It is he who can set our feet in a new and fruitful path. If one were asked which of the books of the last ten years is likely to be regarded in the future as the greatest literary monument of our day, this is the work one might name. As yet only the first six of the thirteen promised volumes are published. These are quite enough to show that our tortured generation has produced a veritable masterpiece of historical interpretation, written by one who is before all things a historian. His range of knowledge is so immense as to be daunting. He is equally at home among the ancient and rather obscure civilisations of Ceylon, China and Easter Island as he is in fields more familiar to us all, ancient Greece and modern America. He does not follow the chronological method, he jumps, at first rather bewilderingly, between B.C. and A.D. and from one side of the world to another, but as one reads on no doubt is left as to what the Professor is trying to do. He is trying to discover from a philosophical study of history in its many facets and scenes what the immense story is all about. He, therefore, regards the objective facts from the point of view of one who indeed has forgotten more history than most of the rest of us have ever learned, but who is, none the less, consciously arguing neither as a historian nor a Christian, but as a scientific objective philosopher who has really mastered the raw material of his trade.

His purpose is, as has been said, to discover what the human story is all about and what is the primary urge behind all the suffering, all the glory, all the treachery and all the heroism which make the stuff of the history books. His answer is un-hesitating and swift : it is the struggle of men and women to create the civilisation of their dreams and to make of themselves the kind of individuals who can fitly be citizens of this per-fected commonwealth. Civilisation is the hero of the piece. The Professor is too wary to define anywhere (at least in his first six volumes) pre-cisely what he means by civilisation. But he leaves us in no doubt that it has little or nothing to do with mechanical contrivances, with com-fort, or even with security. It is a quality of living and, as a social state, that condition which best guarantees to its citizens the freedom within which they may learn to live richly and with grace.

But he does not merely examine his theme in order to discern what its purpose is. He goes deeper and examines it in order to discover the conditions which make the approach to that purpose possible, and the circumstances which impel men to set out on a quest for civilisation which, in each of its stages, is in some degree agonising. History, he says, moves in a vast rhythm. There is first of all the inertia of pre-history, inert precisely because we know little about it : if men had not been inert we should know more. That inertia is broken and in some form or another a challenge is offered to the innate laziness of men, which, because it involves tension and suffering, impels them to struggle to overcome it and thus in their struggle to mount higher on the mountain of Parnassus than they were before the challenge came to them. Progress is, therefore, the result of discomfort and proceeds by a series of jerks. Humanity is woken up out of its long comfortable sleep again. Eventually it dozes again, and, after another spell, there comes a new challenge to wake us all up and force us to struggle still further. Progress is thus a painful thing. The professor isolates the time at which humanity received a special shock ; it is four thousand years before Christ, in some ways the most important date in history. Then something happened, no one can tell what, but men everywhere received some portentous shock which woke them up and set them on the march. Since that time mankind has put forth no less than twenty-one civilising efforts. To this all races but one in the world have made their contribution and that one, the negroid, has still time. The fret and the fever of an enforced wakefulness has never left human beings since that date six thousand years ago.

A primary conclusion at once emerges. If history has any meaning at all, then there is truly such a thing as destiny. That destiny is the perfected civilisation. If Professor Toynbee is right, and it would need uncommon hardihood to contradict him, it follows that the totalitarians have erred in supposing that this destiny is properly thought of as affecting the smaller groups of mankind, such as classes or nations. If destiny is toward civilisation, and if history is any guide at all to the condition of progress, the civilising destiny of mankind is to be thought of as the movement of groups much larger than nations or classes. It may be true that here and there there have been considerable civilising efforts involving a comparatively limited amount of people, as, for example, that of the Polynesian Society, but the normal, identifiable civilisation is a thing far wider than any nation can compass.

The group for example, to which we ourselves belong, which is called generally " The Western Civilisation," is comprised of all those nations which derive their traditions from Greek thought, Roman law, and the Christian revelation. Its boundaries are no less than the whole of Western Europe, stretching out far beyond to the East, to include Greece, and to the West, to include North America. From this we may see that it is nonsense to take history and build upon it a case which produces a destiny for Germany, Italy, Japan, or Russia, and which can only propose for other nations and classes within the same group the task of a slavish subservience to them. Whatever history may or may not mean, at least it cannot mean that.

Christian thought, however, still remains dissatisfied. There is, it will feel, something more to be said before Professor Toynbee can be considered to cast any real light upon the specifically Christian ideas of destiny. The professor says it by going back on his tracks to ask the question, " What woke the slumbering Colossus six thousand years ago ? " Something must have happened to wake him who had slept so peacefully for so long. And since that event happened in the days before written records could exist, it is impossible to produce evidence of what the titanic event was which shook all men everywhere. This question Professor Toynbee turns round and round, and cannot find an answer. If he cannot find it, it means that there is no answer which men can find. He is therefore driven to assume some kind of spiritual interference or intervention, operating from and in the realm in which the Divine exists, and set in motion by the Divine dissatisfaction with His own created handiwork.

This is, of course, an assumption born of the inability to explain facts otherwise. Once, however, you have made it there is a very great deal of evidence that comes in to support it. This is the evidence of every religious mythology in the history of the world. Whether the mythology is a very primitive one, like the first chapter of Genesis or some of the stories of the Greek hero gods, or whether, on the other hand, it is a most subtle and profound legend, like the story of Job, its fundamentals are always the same. They suggest that God made the world and then, for some unexplained reason, evil entered unto it and caused the sleep of inertia. Then God, desiring that His creation should be the best that was possible for it, and perceiving that things were not going as He hoped, Himself descended from his watching throne and challenged the devil to mortal combat on the scene of God's creation, the world. The result of this titanic conflict is naturally the extreme discomfort of all those who are onlookers, and when it begins it is no longer possible for men and women to slumber in peace. So before it is possible to explain why men subject themselves to these agonies and terrors in their search for what is better it is necessary to assume God. And, in exactly the same way, God has to be assumed as the goal of progress, or otherwise it could have none. If God appears, so to speak, at both ends of the scale of time, it is at least likely that He is reasonably to be sought at any moment in the course of it.

Hence, from Professor Toynbee's account we are led to the second conclusion. Destiny is real, but it is bound up with the action of God. He inspires man's search for it and He is the rewarder of those that finish their course, and He only can sustain men as they march. Here is the Christian position profoundly reinforced, while the wrong and, in its results, damnable conception of destiny is condemned not by one who is suspect through writing and thinking as a Christian, but by the most detached and most expert of all living historical philosophers. He is led by a purely scientific and objective study of the facts to the Christian conception of life, in which religion and history build up each other.

In a day when the study of history is so profoundly influential, this is the really fruitful line of apologetic. It is to argue for the necessity of the Christian interpretation of life in such a way as not to demand faith first of all for its acceptance, and yet to retain the overshadowing category of mystery, the abandonment of which always makes nonsense of any scheme of the interpretation of history. Only thus can we still keep the conception of destiny and purge it of the horrible crimes committed in its name.

CHAPTER VI

TRAGEDY AND THE GOSPEL

A JUST consideration of history can thus take us some of the way to finding the answer to the assertions of tragedy and fatalism, but only in the Gospel of Jesus Christ can the moralist really stand on firm ground. His problem is so to face the facts of evil as to wring from them a reasoned hope and a sure faith in the victory of good and in the power of man to escape from his prison of circumstance.

The Gospel story is itself a tragedy, but a tragedy of a unique kind, which makes all the difference. It is a conflict of good with good, worked out in characters of heroic stature. Jesus is confronted by the Pharisees and their way of life and standard of values. They stood for something both great and good. Politically they were the heirs of the Maccabees, the heroic leaders of one of the bravest and most successful revolts against powerful tyranny the world has seen. In the religious sense they were the trustees and exponents of the ancient Law, given under Moses and reformed under Josiah, which had made Israel what it was, held its people together through all their troubles, and enabled them to make their supreme contribution to the common heritage of mankind. The fact that the Pharisees had earned all our Lord's condemnations by their misinterpretation and misuse of the Law does not alter the value of the Law. They were its heirs and its guardians, universally acknowledged as such. Jesus was judged, condemned and crucified by the Roman power represented in the governor, Pontius Pilate, and the Roman Empire was one of the two or three greatest institutions the world has ever seen. There is no doubting the tradition of goodness, the actual greatness, and the heroic stature of the forces opposed to Jesus in the tragic conflict of the Gospel. The sense of pitiful waste is no less deeply stamped on the pages of the Gospel, for it was the record of Israel's refusal of the meaning of all its long history. Our Lord Himself showed His own consciousness of this sad sense of waste as He wept over Jerusalem : " If thou hadst known, even thou, at least in this thy day, the things that belong unto thy peace, but now they are hid from thine eyes."

But at this point the kinship of the Gospel

with Shakespearian tragedy ends and the differences begin. The evil is not visibly destroyed
within the action of the drama. Caiaphas, Pilate
and Herod have their way with Jesus, but, unlike
Iago or Macbeth, the story ends with the Ascen-
sion and leaves them still sitting unmoved in the
seats of the mighty. But if the evil is not visibly
destroyed within the scope of the dramatic action,
destroyed that is in the physical death or visible
defeat of its progenitors, it is spiritually destroyed
actually before it has gained its full physical
victory. Evil was defeated at the moment when
Jesus, instead of cursing His enemies, prayed for
their forgiveness, and at that moment Jesus had
still the worst of His sufferings before Him.
Furthermore, just as the dramatic action of the
Gospel reaches out beyond the Cross to the
Resurrection, so it is impossible to separate Good
Friday from Easter Day. They are different
scenes within a single unity of tragic drama. Thus
the struggle ends with the defeat of evil and the
cost has been the life of the best, but the stage is
not left peopled by mediocrities. The main
actors of the conflict are still in possession of the
stage when the evangelists bring down the cur-
tain. Their stature has been subtly changed, but
they are all there and so the sense of waste, while

certainly present, does not take on the all-pervading, irremediable aspect which it has in a King Lear or a Hamlet.

The difference in atmosphere, however, between the Gospel and classical tragedy goes deeper still. Over classical tragedy there broods an overwhelming sense of fate. All is fated. Nothing takes place as apart from the fate. In no real sense is any one of the characters free to choose his path. He speaks the lines and performs the acts which the fate dictates to him, and if he struggles against his powerlessness the struggle is vain from the start. In the Gospel there is neither hint nor trace of anything of the kind. The story of Jesus Christ is a tragedy with fate left out and God inserted in its place. Its Hero is the master, not the slave of circumstances. The times are out of joint and He comes to set them right, and yet He is at all points free to refuse the mission, free to decide for Himself how to discharge it, able to be tempted to perform His office in the easy and uncreative way of immediately satisfying the popular expectation we had of the Messiah. The life of Jesus moves slowly towards its culmination in the most dreadful of deaths, but it does so by His deliberate choice—a choice He could revoke at any moment.

Professor Vincent Taylor, in his *Jesus and His Sacrifice*, leaves no possible doubt in any reader's mind as he interprets the resolve of Jesus about the Cross. The end was implicit in the beginning, not because circumstances made it so but because Jesus chose it so. He did not face the Cross, but deliberately envisaged and embraced it from the very beginning of His ministry. The Crucifixion was inevitable because His mind had chosen it and for no other reason. It was not fated, not destined, but embraced by the calm, free choice of a human will. The Cross, indeed, is almost as much the defeat of fatalism as it is the defeat of sin.

Christianity is the answer, and the only answer, to the tragic interpretation of life. What makes tragedy intolerable, in spite of its grandeur and its high view of human worth, is the spirit of fatalism that surrounds it. If all is fate, there is simply no room for hope and no rational ground for faith. But if what the evangelists claim for Christ is true, and because, claiming it, they set out their claim in a piece of tragic history of a new and unique kind, then we have the answer to tragedy, and hope and faith are brought back to the world. They come back in the new view of man, which takes away nothing of the greatness which Shakespeare saw in him, but adds that which makes him "but little lower than the angels." In the Gospel all the facts of cosmic and human evil are faced and mastered. The enemy that is overcome is, in the first instance, fatalism, the scourge of humanity in every generation where it gets a hold. And this is the victory, that out of a tragedy is wrung the assertion that a man *is* the master of his soul and the captain of his fate, that he *is* responsible for his life and what he does with it, that he *can* properly be charged with this responsibility because he is free, and that his freedom is precisely freedom from the domination of any fate, or even of any God.

So far, however, we have seen the story of the historic Jesus as the supreme, unique tragedy in which the doubts and problems of classical tragedy are turned aside and answered. One theory has been answering to another, and though this line of thought contributes immensely to our intellectual understanding of the nature of evil, it is still an intellectual theory and not yet a Gospel. What turns it into a Gospel?

The effect of the Gospel is to accept the tragic interpretation of life but to destroy the brooding fatalism of tragedy. This is developed from an intellectual theory into a Gospel able to be received as the authentic Good News by all ordinary men and women everywhere by the addition of three assertions about life which the Gospel makes.

(1) The first assertion is the offer of conversion. There are a few naturally Christian souls for whom, as far as we can see, no process of conversion seems to be necessary. They have " got there " from the beginning, and they pass steadily and with no apparent effort through all the stages of Christian development. St. John, the Beloved Disciple, was such a one, and all of us have known examples here and there. But these people are few. For most of us, as for St. Peter, a more wracking and catastrophic conversion is necessary, and continues to be necessary as Christ comes and knocks on the doors of all the rooms of the house of our life in turn, and we struggle to keep each successive door closed to Him and then painfully open it. From " crisis to crisis advancing " is the line of development of the ordinary Christian soul. The promise of the Gospel is that every conversion is a factor in the defeat of evil and the reversal of the meaning and the value of its consequences. The gift of the Gospel is its assurance of penitence which makes

conversion possible. When and as men and women change sides in the process of the trial, as, that is to say, they are converted, the sting is gradually taken out of evil and life gradually ceases to be tragic.

(2) In opposition to the unheeding, unhelpful and utterly fatalistic deity of classical tragedy, the Gospel speaks of a God of whom Jesus Christ is the picture in terms of flesh. The rules of this queer game we call life will probably always defeat the attempt of the philosophers and artists to make sense of them and to wring from them the ground of a reasoned hope for the players. Why should there be evil in the world? Why does God allow the devil to trouble the earth? How can He be both loving and omnipotent when His world is what it is? Was there no other way but the suffering of human beings to ensure a developing universe? Is it fair that God should provide Himself with the opportunity to exercise His art of continual acts of re-creation at the expense of the pain of humanity, which alone calls the divine act into being? There is probably no really satisfying, no logically impregnable answer to such questions as these. It is, after all, the business of religion to deal in mystery, and every religious question that a man can ask, no

matter how simple, ultimately leads to mystery, the unknown realm where, for the present, a reverent agnosticism is the only possible attitude. Any religion which claims to be able to give a nice pat answer to every question that can be asked exposes itself as a fake. On any showing, the rules of the game of life are quite unfair, and it has successfully puzzled the wisest minds of all the ages to say what God is, so to speak, playing at. But whatever those rules are, and however bitterly unfair they are, it is the message of the Gospel that God freely chose to come into the game of life as a player, to enjoy no single advantage not open to other players, to abide by the rules of the game, fair or unfair, and to take the consequences. The consequences for Him were more dreadful by far than they are for most of the rest of us, and if the rules of life are unfair to us they were ten times more unfair to Him. Nor is the suffering of Calvary for Him an event in history, long over and done with. The mode of His ministry is the eternal self-disclosure of the attitude of the Creator to His creatures. As they suffer, so does He. The Cross is the symbol of God's action now. It cost Him all that suffering then and to redeem us today costs Him no less.

This really does take the sting out of tragedy,

as we may see when we think of the famous end of *Tess of the D'Urbervilles*. The novel is a true tragedy. There is conflict, waste, suffering, a purging of the evil, and Tess herself, if not Angel Clare, is of heroic stature. At last Tess is hanged in Winchester Prison, and Hardy's comment on his tale is one of the most famous sentences in all literature : " ' Justice ' was done, and the President of the Immortals, in Æschylean phrase, had ended his sport with Tess." There has never been a more bitter accusation hurled in the teeth of God, and if classical tragedy is the only answer to the challenge of evil, every word of that bitter cry is justified. But it is not the only answer. A Christian is fully entitled to take Hardy's cry of protest and paraphrase it thus, " The President of the Immortals had ended his sport with Christ." that is with Himself. He leads us through no darker room than He went through before.

(3) Hardy's Tess can best introduce us to the third assertion of the Gospel which changes a theory into an evangel. Immediately after the famous taunt at God, quoted above, Hardy adds, " And the d'Urberville knights and dames slept on in their tomb unknowing." This refers back to the last talk that Tess and Angel had together as they waited by Stonehenge for her arrest. All

her doubts but one were resolved. She had no fear but one, and to that one her talk at last turned. " Tell me now, Angel, do you think we shall meet again after we are dead ? I want to know." To avoid replying he kissed her. " O, Angel—I fear that means no," said she with a suppressed sob. " And I wanted so to see you again —so much, so much ! What—not even you and I, Angel, who love each other so well ? " But no answer came, for unadorned tragedy can give none. " The rest is silence." The Gospel meets this need by its message of the resurrection to the life of the world to come and its bestowal of immortality upon human spirits not as a right but as a gift of God. The virtue of this promise as the final answer to tragedy does not lie in any idea of bringing other worlds into existence to redress the balance of this world. We have to set about the defeat of evil in the here and now. It lies, on the contrary, in the fact that it exactly contradicts the spirit of Hardy's final ejaculation of despair, about the d'Urberville knights sleeping unknowing in their tombs, by making possible the doctrine of the Communion of Saints, with all it implies. It places the individual and the community upon a real equality and so gives the clue to the only conceivable solution to the tension existing between them. Since it is from this tension that most tragic circumstances are derived this is relevant indeed. To be assured, as the Gospel emphatically assures us, of resurrection to eternal life, is to be given at last the hope and the promise that the slow wasteful ways in which sinful men are bound to bring in the Kingdom of God are not the rules of the final reality of living.

CHAPTER VII

THE SIN AGAINST THE HOLY GHOST

THE purpose of the preceding chapters has been to try to take the measure of evil as an abstract, spiritual force, to discover what its strategy must be, and to find out the laws which govern its growth, decline and fall. Its purpose, as we saw, must be rather to take good and spoil it rather than to take wickedness and intensify it. World affairs at present give an unwontedly vivid picture of the devil at work, and from a study of them we learn that primary consequence of satanic energy is sheer confusion, ethical terms losing all meaning, history becoming strictly nonsensical, the whole life and effort of men cracking at the centre of his building by the disintegration of sheer contradiction. The logical end and the final victory of evil is the enthronement of Nihilism as the chief principle of living. Its chief weapon is the attack on truth. But at every stage of this process good takes up the challenge and the artists draw the picture of this conflict in classical tragedy. Though the effect of tragedy is the defeat of evil, and the assertion of the greatness of man, it raises more questions than it answers, and it leaves any sensitive person still more rebellious against the nature of things than he was before. From this dilemma the Gospel rescues us by taking ethical terms and values and firmly planting them in the supernatural soil where alone they can flourish, by clearly demonstrating that the weakness of evil is that it can succeed only on success and never on failure, by rescuing us from the gloomy and ultimately damnable religion of fatalism, which, apart from the God of the Gospel, is the only dignified answer to the challenge of evil, and by taking away the sin of the world through the Cross of Christ.

Having tried to master the theory of evil, and of good in conflict with it, the next step is obvious. A man must apply it to his own soul, for he cannot repent of the sins of someone else, or of the sins of society, until he has first repented of his own. This naturally involves a constant self-examination—an activity of the soul which, as it is strengthened by a widening knowledge of the ways of evil and of God's love as answering it, reaches ever deeper into the levels of consciousness. It is the sin of which we are not conscious, and so is never repented of, that does the real mischief. Half the teaching of Christ is a set of variations on just this theme, and they are all brought together in the story of the Publican and the Pharisee who went down to the Temple to pray. The foregoing discussion, however, should have provided some principles of personal self-examination which can help to save us from complacency, the deadliest of all sins, and from the inevitable doom pronounced on the unexamined life.

The Gospel firmly embeds ethical terms and values in a setting of supernatural religion, and thus provides them with the only ground on which they can stand. But the devil, attacking the concept of abstract truth, roots them out again, so that they become hopelessly confused and contradictory and lead straight to a topsy-turvy, nihilistic world. Hence the first principle of him who would save his soul alive must be to call evil things evil and good things good, and to allow no consideration of contingency to blur the distinction. This is by no means easy, for in a naughty world contingency is bound to play a big part, and the Christian cannot escape it. The present war, for instance, is like all other wars, an utterly evil thing, but the contingency of circumstances is such that most Christians sincerely believe it their Christian duty to take part in it. It is, for them, a lesser evil than refusing their part. But, none the less, war is evil, and a Christian's soul is in mortal danger if he forgets it.

The failure to call a good thing good and an evil thing evil was called by our Lord the sin against the Holy Ghost for which there can be no forgiveness. He had just healed a man and the Pharisees said that He did it in the power of Beelzebub. His reply was that this suggested that the devil fought against himself, which is unlikely. It was also to say of a plainly good thing that it was bad. He added, in Dr. Temple's paraphrase,[1] " Say what you like about me (whoso speaketh a word against the Son of Man it shall be forgiven him), but if when the very spirit of goodness is plainly at work before you, you call it bad because it happens not to fit into your scheme, then there is really no hope. (Whoso speaketh against the Holy Ghost, it shall not be forgiven him either in this world, nor in the world to come.)" It comes to this : to call a plainly good thing bad because you don't approve of the people who did it, or the way they did it, or the cause in which it

[1] *The Faith and Modern Thought.* William Temple. (Macmillan). P. 95.

was done, is as serious a sin as a man can commit. And the reverse is equally true. It is a sin against the Holy Ghost to take a plainly bad thing and call it good because you approve of the people who did, or the cause for which they did it. When this happens ethical terms have lost all meaning and the devil's victory is here.

Partisanship is the chief temptation which leads us to commit this sin, and of such a partisanship Europe has been full for a long time. For a concentration of sheer satanic wickedness the Spanish Civil War was hard to beat. Yet every vile thing that was then done found some onlookers to hail it as good. The reaction of extreme Right Wing in English politics to the wickedness of the Gestapo, and of the Left Wing (particularly among the Bloomsbury Intellectuals) to the equally vile wickedness of the Ogpu in Russia, is another instance of the same blindness. Whether in politics or in private life, it is disconcertingly easy to commit the sin against the Holy Ghost. Every time a man deals mercilessly with a sin to which he happens to have no temptation, and all too lightly with a sin which happens also to be his own, he has set his feet on this fatal road. The best guard against it is to make up one's mind once and for all that since partisanship must needs be, one will judge one's own side and one's own cause with an even greater severity than one applies to the judgment of the opponent. When trade unionists are even more eloquent about the shortcomings of Trade Unions than they are about those of the Federation of British Industries, and *vice versâ*, we shall have a society in which the devil will not find it easy to get a foothold.

Our Lord had very much to say about the pre-conditions of evil's success, and those who wish to help in the mastery of evil must take Him seriously. There is no need to suppose that in His injunction to the rich young ruler to sell all that he had and give to the poor He meant His words to be taken by everyone with a slavish literalness. Obviously, such a universality as this would be impossible, and, in its consequences, immoral. But there can be no possible doubt that He did regard wealth and too high a standard of comfort and security with a real hostility. Un-questionably He would have echoed St. Paul's remark, " The love of money is a root of most evil!" Recent history again furnishes the apt commentary. The most notable feature of this war has been the prevalence of treachery. It would be hard to name a more odious and contemptible crime. But those who have been guilty of it have one and all been drawn from those social circles where resistance to evil has been sapped by too much wealth and too much comfort; and their motives, so far as one can yet estimate them, have been the determination to preserve for themselves at any cost the wealth and power and comfort they had.

Yet, and here is an illustration of how evil constantly overreaches itself, this inordinate love of money and ease produces the conditions where neither have meaning. If today as we wait in England to be invaded, and stand, as we know, in a greater danger than any generation of Englishmen has ever faced, and yet find a deep exhilaration and a real sense of freedom in the midst of the ordeal, it is because circumstances have freed us from the bondage of our fealty to money and to ease. Against an inordinate love of money and an over-valuation of ease and security, Jesus warned us again and again. We did not heed His warning, and our idolatry inevitably led us by way of the economic crisis into war. Yet the war has meant that our security has completely vanished, our wealth is fast becoming meaningless, and our ease, if we have any, is a burden. Few of us miss any one of them, but feel far freer than before.

What is happening is that today we are being forced by circumstances to live as though the Christian scale of material values was true, and we find that the result is a new exhilaration and freshness, that we are made more fully members one of another, and that the gate has been opened to the entry of the Holy Spirit, who, as so many signs and portents show, is today " cloaking our people with a rich embrace."

CHAPTER VIII

THE SOCIETY FOR CORPORATE PENITENCE

ONE of the age-old dilemmas of the Christian who must try to live as a Christian in the midst of a world which is so largely an organised repudiation of Christianity has come upon us today with renewed force. In the circumstances of 1940 how is a Christian to hate the sin and love the sinner? How do we love the people who do hateful things? There is no manner of doubt that this is the duty laid upon him by Christ, and he is in no way exempted from discharging it by the fact that his nation is at war. But how in actual practice is he to love the sinner and repudiate the sin he commits? When he tries, does it not often come to this, that he seeks to show his love for the sinner by making excuses for the sin he commits and trying to convince himself that after all it is not as sinful as it sounds. But to pretend that an outrage is not outrageous because one wants to think of its perpetrator as a Christian should is neither to repudiate the sin

nor to love the sinner. An honest straightfor-
ward hatred of the sinner is better than that, for
at least that does not play false to our ethical
standards. Yet there must be some better way.

Let us imagine two men, one of them an
ordinary, decent fellow, but not a Christian, and
the other one who learns the art of living from
Christian sources and consciously struggles to
rule his life in accordance with his understanding
of them. For some years both have had a very
painful time with the daily newspaper and the
broadcast news. One morning both of them
open their papers and they read of some ghastly
outrage, it may be the Nazi Purge of June 1934,
or the Rape of Guernica, or the bombing of
Helsinki, or the Massacre of Rotterdam. Heaven
knows, there are plenty of examples. The first
man is utterly horrified. He is all blazing with
pity for the victims of the outrage. He burns to
give its perpetrators a taste of their own medicine.
He longs for punishment. Then his thoughts go
deeper. He feels somehow that he is personally
dirtied in this dirtying of humanity, for after all
those who do such things are of the same type
and species as himself. But, and here is the curse
of it, he quickly realises that, resent it as he may,
there is really nothing that he can do about it.

There it is, a fact he cannot alter, a weight of unmerited human suffering he can do little or nothing to redeem, and, for himself, a whole mass of tormenting emotions for which he can find no outlet. He is oppressed by his utter helplessness. The next time he reads of such an outrage his reactions are a little less violent, and little by little his conscience is numbed precisely by his sense of helplessness, and he ends by sadly accepting outrage as very regrettable but quite inevitable. Alternately, he may refuse to accept his sense of helplessness. His emotions cannot be stifled. They must find an utterance. Thus he will make violent and bitter speeches, denouncing the " Thrice Perjured Traitors," which, although they may well contain accusations strictly true, only form the prelude to yet more affronts of the same kind. Alternatively, he will clamour for economic sanctions, for reprisals, or for war. His will be the voice of the natural man whose emotion is indeed commendable, since it is unbearable wrong that engenders it.

But very swiftly instinct will predominate over reason, and the practical result of this self-directed sense of humiliation is in fact merely to increase the very weight and number of the outrages on common decency which caused it in the first instance. Humiliation of this sort has nothing redemptive about it : it merely adds to its own stature. It may be called by the name of penitence, but actually it leads directly away from penitence, never towards it. For however just and however sacrificial the indignant humiliation of this first man may be, as long as he thinks of the sin in question as primarily an affront to " our common humanity " it will not occur to him that he has any share in it, and that the call to corporate penitence is a cry which demands his response no less truly than the response of those he rightly denounces. For the modern civilisation of the West is one and indivisible, and though the pace in wickedness is at present being set by only a part of it, it is the whole of it and not merely the one area of specially deep infection which is being brought to judgment. In this sense it is true that the world is what it is, not because a very few are monstrously wicked, but because most of us are what we are. The last state of that man is worse than the first. For all his honest rage he has done much less than nothing to redeem the evil he rightly denounces.

The second man, the Christian, reads the tale of the same outrages in the same paper. His disgust is not less than the first's, though he is a little less shocked because the doctrine of Original Sin has taught him something of the depth of depravity into which human beings can fall. He, too, is intensely moved by the innocent suffering involved. But for him the outrage is primarily an outrage against God, and only secondarily against its immediate victims.

It is an affront to God. God's universal love is being flouted, His mercy denied and His principle of the sacredness of personality derided. God gives all and we take His good and perfect gifts and use some to beggar half our population in the unemployment and under-employment of economic insecurity, and others to provide ambition with its propaganda and the lust for power with its armoury. It is an outrage, but primarily the outrage is directed against God and only incidentally against man.

The second man, who is distressed and humiliated most of all because God's love is being refused, is in the healthier state. Though indignation and righteous anger will be present in his mind, sorrow will be yet more deeply rooted, and therefore he will be delivered from the temptation to relieve the turmoil in his heart by looking around for a scapegoat to bear it for him. Instead, he will look first into his own soul and see if some part of the evil he is plainly bound to condemn in others has not found a lodgment there. He will realise, too, that while it is a part of the condemnation of evil force that it has to be fought with its own weapons at first, yet it is by opposing evil with good that the final victory is won. And he will not see in such statements merely the platitudes of piety, as will the first man, for he will be a Christian, and as such he will anchor his sorrow to the Divine Rock of Supernatural Grace.

The second man, in fact, is delivered from the sense of agonising and ultimately dulling helplessness of the first. To drop bombs on the children of a nation with whom one is not even at war is a ghastly outrage which he cannot possibly imagine he would himself commit. But if it is not primarily an outrage against the children who are killed or maimed but against God, well, he knows very well that he, too, outrages God's love every day of his life. He knows also that he is not helpless when he does. There is the whole range of contrition, penitence, confession, absolution and restoration open for him to use.

The difficulty is that those who commit the sort of outrages against God's love which get into the newspapers, the public atrocities so to speak, are commonly quite unable to repent for themselves. It is hard to think of a single totalitarian statesman, for example, to whom the whole language of this book would not be utterly unmeaning. But the Christian religion clearly answers the difficulty when it teaches that vicarious sacrifice is acceptable before God and constitutes a currency which He can accept in payment of the bill He is bound to present to the world for the sins it commits. We believe that Jesus Christ died for the sins of the world, and that the Cross does for us what we could never have done for ourselves in that it justifies the penitent before God and enables God to receive and forgive him. Christ did not consult the people for whom He died to ask them whether they would wish Him to do this for them. He simply did it, and because He did it we are able to be forgiven. In Him the principle of vicarious sacrifice is clearly established and it is the only possible way out of the difficulty we are considering. They cannot repent, these Hitlers and Himmlers, for they simply do not know what the word means. Therefore we must repent for them as well as for ourselves. If we do not, it simply means that their crimes go unrepented like so many bills delivered to humanity which are never paid. Unpaid bills of this kind simply mean that humanity is leaving more and more fields to be occupied by the devil and evil is allowed to have a free course.

It is no doubt true that no man may deliver his brother, but if that means that my confession of the sins that Hitler sees no reason to confess for himself is utterly unavailing both for the good of his soul and for the defeat of evil, it is hard to make sense of the Atonement, and harder still to think that the common demand for corporate repentance is anything more than a fine phrase. We do not claim that this sort of vicarious repentance results in the complete deliverance of the brother for whom it is made, but merely that it does somehow benefit him and that the train of evil which he is laying does somehow receive a check. In any case we are moving here in a field of mystery where precise language is not possible. But it does not seem logical to tell me to pray for Hitler and assure me that my prayers for him have a real effect, and then to forbid me to offer to God an act of penitence in his stead. If we must say the prayers which he and his kind leave unsaid then we must also do the acts of penitence which he leaves undone. The teaching of Christ, by word and by act, covers and justifies both undertakings and inferentially, if not explicitly, commands them.

That is, however, more properly a matter for the theologians and so outside the scope of this book. What is within it is the question of purging evil in a particularly horrible form by the positive glory of the Christian faith. We started by noting the extreme difficulty of loving the sinner and hating the sin in the circumstances of 1940. The difficulty we have now resolved. I cannot more wholeheartedly repudiate a sin than I do by regarding it as an outrage against God and by going on my knees to make an act of penitence for it. I cannot more truly express my love for the sinner who commits it than I do by taking the trouble to pay so much of his ethical account as I can and asking that at any rate a part of this sin be not put to his charge. No doubt such a practice can very easily become a mere formality, but that is true of every other religious practice. It is simply necessary to see that the contrition is real and not formal. There is a piece of help which can here be given. The nearer the act of penitence comes to the first reading of the outrage which calls for it the more real and the less formal will it be. It must follow the news as quickly as possible. It is best to make an act of penitence and beseech God's forgiveness within five minutes of first hearing of the outrage. That is to say, that one does it within the space of time that one's initial shock, horror and indignation are still hot and burning. If the penitence be put off until one's evening prayers it is very difficult indeed to prevent it from being purely formal. In this, as in our own private confessions, the only unreality is the unreality of offering to God a penitence which costs us nothing.

Further, to think and act like this is to save one's own sanity and to keep alive one's own sense of the awfulness of sin. The first man of our parable boiled with fury over the cruel outrage he read of and was swept by pity for its victims. But there was nothing he could do about it and so his emotions seethed within him and could find no outlet. That is always psychologically disastrous. But the Christian ought not to be thus struck dumb and impotent. There should be something of a characteristically Christian and spiritual sort that he can do about it. There is. He can repent of it, though someone else did it.

So far, we have thought chiefly, almost exclusively, in terms of political crime, keeping in mind the atrocities of the great political criminals. But the principle is capable of almost infinite expansion. Hitler is not the only man who commits sins he sees no need to repent. In degree, every man and woman who lives without God in the world does the same and falls within the same category. So do institutions when they act coporately, governments, nations, churches, town councils, local committees—there is no end to it. For every sin that is repented of there are probably twenty that go unshriven. Hence the call for corporate penitence on the part of the nation, and the only way that this call can in fact be answered is if the Church takes upon herself the charge of continuously confessing the sins of the world. The Church, in fact, must be a Society for Corporate Penitence if it is ever to be a Society of Divine Redemption. The call for penitence and the acceptance of God's judgment on the part of a whole civilisation is therefore meaningless unless it is also a call to the Church to see itself as a Society for Corporate Penitence. It becomes the business of the Church to confess all the sins which others do not see the need to confess themselves. It is the dreadful responsibility of the members of the Church to bear and bring before God the guilt of civilisation as well as the smaller and more personal guilt of the sin in their own lives. And this the Church must do amid isolation and misunderstanding, for who but Christians can see any reality in such conceptions as these? But how enormously enriched is so ordinary a piece of liturgical worship as the recitation of the General Confession when it is conceived of as being concerned with the whole sin of an age.

No one can properly be a member of a society for Corporate Penitence who does not see his membership as constituting a crushing burden, a veritable calvary which he can bear only by constant discipline and by an unfettered use of the full tale of his emotional and spiritual resources. For no repentance is real unless there is agony in it, and the sin of an age, constantly repeated, is not something one can repent at once and then it is over. If I commit a sin I can repent of it, confess it, and be forgiven. There is agony in that if there is also sincerity, but for one sin I need only make one act of repentance. But the deeper life of penitence has no end till God's Kingdom comes, and it is to that deeper and more costly penitence for the sin of a civilisation that God calls the Church and her children to-day.

Such a penitence as this has to be expressed both in worship and in life, and it cannot be expressed in life, or what is called "practical action," until it has first of all been expressed in worship, for worship is the symbol or the concentration of the theocentric life. A Society for Corporate Penitence has its being first of all in liturgical places. No one can take his place in a society such as this until he has learned that every form of liturgical confession is as truly corporate as personal, that every time he comes before the Throne of Grace to say "We have sinned" he is thinking at least as much of the corporate sin of his own civilisation as of the personal sin of which his own conscience makes him bitterly aware. Such worship as this removes every imputation of unintelligibility or unreality from its forms of expression, for it is deliberately anchoring itself to the evil all around, than which nothing could be more grimly real, and also to the Supreme Reality whose Name is Mercy. It stretches out one hand to the frantic misery of our evil age and the other to the God who is burning to help and save. It forms a link between the two, and joins them together, pressing the sinful weakness of our civilisation close to God's strength. A Church which thinks of itself in its worshipping, liturgical life as a Society for giving expression to the penitence of those who do not even know what the word means, is making it possible for them to be forgiven. Thus—and only thus—it becomes the Forgiving Society, which, as the Body of Christ, is its fundamental title and mission.

But as in worship so in life, for all life is worship. A Society for Corporate Penitence cannot dissolve when its liturgical worship is done and its members come out of church. The process by which it makes possible the redemption of an age is also the process by which it is itself keyed to live on a higher plane of creative fellowship with Society. Unless the members of the Society for Corporate Penitence also conceive of themselves as the storm troopers of the Kingdom of God on earth, and set about the redemption of every field of self-expression in the civilisation of which they are a part, all that is said and done in church is so much mockery. But the God whom they beseech to forgive the world in answer to their ceaseless penitential pleading of Christ's Sacrifice for it, is also the God who through the Holy Spirit inspires them with energy, judgment and love, and enormously enlarges their horizons of the practical. A real sincerity and a ceaseless tirelessness in the one activity is the guarantee of effectiveness in the other.

The great masters of the spiritual life have always pointed out that there is a sense in which penitence is a joyful activity. They meant by that to point to the joy of knowing absolution. But they also meant something deeper, that the exercise of the penitential spirit brings us face to face with God's creative energy and enables us to absorb it. Thus only can sinful men really go on their way rejoicing and with hope, and their joy and hope are the fruits of God's Grace, which their penitence alone enables them to receive. A Society for Corporate Penitence is a joyful society because its members know that it is a Society of Enablement. They are all the time paying the price of those sins, both corporate and personal, which are unrepented of, and so all the time freeing the channel of God's Grace from the blockage which stops it up. It is this activity which is prior to everything else because it is central to everything else. There will be no question of building a new and less ungodly civilisation until all those who love God and know what penitence is are found constantly on their knees taking upon themselves, so far as human beings can, the burden of the evil of our present civilisation.

It is only the penitent who can see with God's

eyes, and it is only to " the worm that knows it is a worm that God gives wings." Nor ought it to be impossible or extravagant to the Christian to make himself a worm for the future's sake. For penitence, whether personal or vicarious, brings us face to face with the Cross, and in the light that shines from the Cross we can at least see clearly and with hope. The cross is the condition of hope. Without it the bravest can see nothing but ruin and desolation ahead. With it we are made one with the pledge of Calvary that triumphant evil digs its own grave. From that titanic conflict, in which evil was victorious, we can see that evil is always subject to the law of diminishing returns and that good alone is exempt from it. And what sets the law of diminishing returns in motion is the faithfulness of Christians. If only we can be true to our Master the building of the new Christian civilisation can begin tomorrow. To oppose all the tremendous forces of evil which have brought Europe to its present pass there are only the prayers, the faith and the love of Christians. But these are enough, if only we believe in them and use them. For they constitute both the petition for God's grace and the ability to receive it, and the Grace of God, even when contained in earthen vessels, is today, as it has always been, the one force which can overwhelm human depravity.

It is because Christians alone understand language like this, and know it to be true, that their responsibility at this present juncture is so tremendous and awe-inspiring. They have in their keeping the only salve for a wounded world, the only way to peace, the only chance that the next civilisation may be less of a bitter tragedy than the last. It is they who, under God, are the real architects of the future. The real test of whether they believe it or not will lie in the readiness they show to undertake the office of the world's penitents. That is their first task—to believe, to practice and to spread penitence. That conditions everything else. All follows from it: without it, nothing can follow.

CHAPTER IX

THE SERENE SOUL

At no point in the Gospel is the Christian given the least encouragement to hope that he may see any result of his labours. If by any chance he does, that is to be regarded as the special mercy of God. But for the most part the strategy of the Church in its conflict with evil is to oppose to its violence a steady, cumulative pressure, composed of the prayers and service, the ethical insights, the vicarious penances, the hope and the faith of the mass of unknown Christians all over the world; and all of it offered to God for Him to add it together, intensify it and make it fruitful. It is all profoundly anonymous and austere, and for that reason it is often exceedingly discouraging. We believe that evil can be mastered, that it has in fact already been mastered potentially by the merits of the Cross. In that belief we try to take our part as members of the society for corporate penitence, and we oppose to it our prayers, our service, our sacrifices and our faith. But from time to time there sweeps over us the depressing realisation that there is very little, if anything, to show for it all. Evil seems to be quite unaffected and the devil goes undisturbed on his way.

That all of us some of the time and some of us most of the time should feel like this is inevitable. If we did not it would merely mean that we were insensitive creatures and those who would fight evil must be highly sensitive to the horror of it. Without this they would quickly give up the fight as hopeless. But this conviction of futility is also dangerous. A soldier must believe in the certainty of victory, and that whatever his present sufferings may be they are worth while because they contribute an essential element of that victory. He must have his inner integrity. He must be serene. It may not be easy in the circumstances of 1940 to remain serenely confident of good's mastery over evil, or to believe that the mite one contributes oneself can have the least effect on the course of the struggle. This, in part, is due to our chronic habit of allowing our minds to be over impressed by mere bulk. In 1940 there is undoubtedly a good deal more evil about than there has been for many years. But in essence the problem of evil and the task of its mastery remain the same whether we are thinking of it in terms of

K 2

the colossal wickedness of this war or in terms of a single crying child waiting drearily in the rain outside the public house in a back street until its parents come out and let it into its home. The rage of heaven is the same whether it is a single crying child or a weeping multitude that it sees.

The problem of the insolence of successful evil is a spiritual problem, and it must be spiritually faced and mastered. There is no lack of precedents to guide us, for this is a problem which has tormented the great souls of all the ages. Perhaps it is dealt with most briefly and memorably in Psalm lxxiii—a psalm which must have come frequently into the minds of many Christians in these days, and comforted them when in their despair they cried, My God, my God, why? The psalm, so the commentators say, belongs to the "Wisdom" literature and period of the Bible, and so expresses a spiritual experience passed in more tranquil external circumstances than fell to the lot of most generations of Jews. It opens with a deliberately conventional and even commonplace ritual acknowledgment of God's goodness.

> Truly God is loving unto Israel : even unto such as are of a clean heart.

But it does not always seem like that, except to those who never think of the meaning of the phrases they use in worship, or who go through life with their eyes shut. And if it now seemed to the psalmist that God was verily and indeed loving unto Israel, it was only through the fires of an agonising period of spiritual despair that he had come to his freedom and serenity. He had walked on the very edge of the precipice. He had almost fallen into the abyss.

> And why ? I was grieved at the wicked :
> I do also see the ungodly in such prosperity.

Look at the world and see how true it is that selfishness pays every time. The wicked are physically strong, they are able to protect themselves against the misfortunes of other decent folk, they can evade the laws because it is their sort that mostly make and administer them. Their immunity leads them to pride, their pride to cruelty and oppression, and their cruelty either to a complete forgetfulness of God or to wild blasphemies against Him. They talk like Rabshakeh talked to Hezekiah, or as the servants of the Evil One soliloquised in the Book of Wisdom, a bitter mocking of God and scorn of those who are still fools enough to serve Him when they so plainly get nothing out of it, and the scales are weighted against them. And the worst of it is that with their wicked blasphemy they corrupt others, having undermined their spiritual resistance by their apparent invulnerability.

> Tush, say they, how should God perceive it ?
> Is there knowledge in the most High ?

There is reason to think that "they" in this verse does not refer to the wicked but to the people in general, to public opinion, which then goes on to draw the inevitable conclusion,

Lo, these are the ungodly, these prosper in the world, and these have riches in possession : and I said,
Then have I cleansed my heart in vain, and washed my hands in innocency.

If the "I" also refers to the people as a whole, it may be doubted how much cleansing of the heart they had really done. But the psalmist, who had made a full and conscientious use of every religious practice, was no less tempted to fling it all away as valueless. Of what use were these prayers and fasts, these services and confessions ? Why bother any more with them ? The wicked think nothing of them and they are lusty and strong.

He was within an ace of denying altogether the

love and the omnipotence of God when the same thought saved him that has since saved thousands of his successors standing miserably in the same spot. Very well, then, deny God. Curse God and die, as Job's wife said. But first think what it involves. It means denying also the faith of the saints. It is to say of this glorious life of my friend, of the whole basis of my mother's existence, of the strength and stay of him who brought me to God, that it is a pure delusion. Yet these things I have seen for myself, and I have *known* them to be true. How can I deny them? No, to deny God or to curse Him is too simple. It does not really solve the problem of evil and it only raises the corresponding problem of good. There is no relief that way. What then? Neither intellect nor heart, it seemed, could bring any relief to this tormenting doubt. There remained only God, and to Him the psalmist must turn again.

Then thought I to understand this : but it was too hard
    for me,
Until I went into the sanctuary of God.

An earlier psalmist had faced the same problem and come to a wildly false conclusion,

Yet never saw I the righteous forsaken, or his seed begging
    their bread.

On which the only possible comment is that either he was a liar or else he was blind. The present psalmist scorns such easy and false conclusions. But the first conclusion he offers is false none the less. He points out that the wicked are not so secure as they think, that in reality they stand on a slippery slope—

> then understood I the end of these men;
> Namely how thou dost set them in slippery places: and castest them down and destroyest them.
> O how suddenly do they consume, perish, and come to a fearful end.

Yes, some do, but not all, not at any rate in this world, and it is in this world that we have to face the challenge of evil. His earlier insight was more true to experience. "They are in no peril of death." Even if the sudden destruction of the wicked was true of every wicked man in the world except one, we would not accept it as a solution. This insight is false: it does not work like that. And this the psalmist sees,

> So foolish was I and ignorant: even as it were a beast before thee.

But his sojourn in the sanctuary of God brought him back to serene peace after all, not by way of an intellectual justification but by his new realisation that nothing that the wicked could do was able to separate him from God. To be with God—that alone mattered, and there alone was peace.

> Nevertheless, I am always by thee : for thou hast holden me by my right hand.
> Thou shalt guide me with thy counsel : and after that receive me with glory.
> Whom have I in heaven but thee : and there is none upon earth that I desire in comparison of thee.
> My flesh and my heart faileth : but God is the strength of my heart, and my portion for ever.

In my own mind, that psalm is always connected with another, the first few verses of psalm 139. It is beyond my commentary or paraphrase :

> O Lord, thou hast searched me out and known me : thou knowest my down-sitting and mine uprising ; thou understandest my thoughts long before.
> Thou art about my path, and about my bed : and spiest out all my ways.
> For lo, there is not a word in my tongue : but thou, O Lord, knowest it all together.
> Thou has fashioned me behind and before : and laid thine hand upon me.
> Such knowledge is too wonderful and excellent for me : I cannot attain unto it.
> Whither shall I go then pass thy Spirit : or whither shall I go then from thy presence ?
> If I climb up into heaven, thou art there : if I go down to hell, thou art there also.

If I take the wings of the morning : and remain in the
  uttermost parts of the sea ;
Even there also shall thy hand lead me; and thy right
  hand shall hold me.

In the whole work of taking into an evil,
hate-causing situation the salve of loving service
whereby the hate is neutralised and the evil
reversed, the ability to withdraw oneself from it
and consciously enter the presence of God is
vital. The alternation of attachment and detachment is the creative rhythm. It was necessary
for Christ Himself periodically to withdraw into
a desert place apart by Himself alone, and it is
ten times as necessary for His disciples. If the
most exacting and exhausting works of mercy
are still left for Christians to perform, it is
mainly because their long training in prayer,
meditation, and worship has taught them that
only in God can they find the strength which
counterbalances the wastage of energy of the
disappointments and the anonymity to which
their work subjects them. Those who would
fling themselves into the fight to master evil
must before all things have their being in heavenly
places.

This is not escapism, or if it is, it is escapism
of the creative sort. Any biblical hero would

have laughed at the idea. For throughout the Bible, in Old and New Testament alike, to come into the sanctuary of God was to enter the place where not only consolation but also energy was to be found. The idea of the presence of God was coupled by every biblical writer with the idea of a surging, restless, illimitable energy. In prayer we are made one with it, and the cells of our endurance are recharged by it, and our consciousness of God's presence is not, in the biblical view, something which lulls us into quiescence, but something which impels us into action.

It is the only road to that serene certitude of mind without which creative work in these fields cannot long be done. To have the knowledge of God, and perpetually to renew it, is to find there today what the saints have always found in the past, the assurance that in spite of everything God reigns, and His will is always vindicated. The defeat of evil and the victory of good is foreordained and inevitable. We can try to serve His purposes and so hasten the day of His complete victory ; or we can delay the day of the consummation of His triumph. But whether we serve Him or deny Him makes no difference to the ultimate reality of things.

It is His Kingdom and not ours. He will bring it to fulfilment, and we can do no more than help or hinder. In all history, it is precisely those who are most of all assured of the fated inevitability of the victory of the cause they serve, who labour yet more abundantly than they all. This they are able to do because their conviction, and their ability perpetually to renew the springs of it, gives to them the invulnerably serene mind which is the first essential of the revolutionary spirit. To undertake to serve in the enterprise of the mastery of evil nothing less than the revolutionary spirit is required.

But that which constitutes its force and its energy is the conviction that God has already done it all. It was His energy that found the way to Calvary, and by His Cross the snare is broken and we are delivered.

THE END

N.B.   *A complete list of volumes in The Christian Challenge Series will be found overleaf.*

THE CHRISTIAN CHALLENGE SERIES

THE KINGDOM OF GOD
By The Very Rev. C. A. Alington, D.D.
THE ACTIVITY OF GOD
By The Bishop of Liverpool
THE PROBLEM OF PAIN
By C. S. Lewis, M.A.
THE APPROACH TO CHRISTIANITY
By Rev. Norman Pittenger, S.T.B.
CHRISTIANITY AND THE NEW PSYCHOLOGY
By Rev. Dr. W. B. Selbie, D.D.
GOD'S DEMAND AND MAN'S RESPONSE
By Rev. Alec R. Vidler, B.D.
THE CRISIS OF THE REFORMATION
By Rev. Dr. Norman Sykes, D.D.
THE CHURCH IN THE ANCIENT WORLD
By Rev. Dr. L. Elliott-Binns, D.D.
GOD, CREATION, AND REVELATION
By Rev. Dr. A. J. Macdonald, D.D.
THE CHRISTIAN HOPE OF IMMORTALITY
By Professor A. E. Taylor, LL.D.
CHRISTIANITY AND OTHER RELIGIONS
By Rev. C. J. Shebbeare, D.D.
CHRISTIAN MORAL CONDUCT
By Rev. A. E. Garvie, M A., D.D.
RELIGION IN SOCIAL ACTION
By Maurice B. Reckitt, M.A.
THE CHRISTIAN DOCTRINE OF GRACE
By Rev. Professor Oscar Hardman, D.D.
THE NEW TESTAMENT PROBLEM
By Rev. L. J. Collins, M.A.
RELIGION AND THE STATE
By Rev. Dr. H. Maurice Relton, D.D.
HISTORY OF CHRISTIAN THOUGHT
By The Very Rev. E. Gordon Selwyn, D.D. (Dean of Winchester)
CHRISTIAN ETHICS AND SOCIAL HEALTH
By Dr. H. P. Newsholme, M.D.
THE DOCTRINE OF THE ATONEMENT
By Rev. Father Lionel Thornton, C.R.
THE ORIGINS OF RELIGION
By Rev. Dr. E. O. James, D.LITT., PH.D.
THEISM, AGNOSTICISM AND ATHEISM
By Edward Ingram Watkin, M.A. (Oxon)
THE DOCTRINE OF THE INCARNATION
By Rev. Dr. J. K. Mozley, D.D.
CHRISTIANITY IN THE SOCIAL STATE
By Rev. Dr. W. F. Lofthouse, D.D.
THE MASTERY OF EVIL
By Rev. Canon Roger Lloyd, M.A.